W9-BHZ-833

HOW TO PLAY
WINNING
POKER

ABOUT THE AUTHOR

Avery Cardoza is the foremost gambling authority in the world and best-selling author of twenty-one gambling books and advanced strategies, including *How to Win at Gambling, Secrets of Winning Slots*, and the classic, *Winning Casino Blackjack for the Non-Counter*.

Cardoza began his gambling career underage in Las Vegas as a professional blackjack player beating the casinos at their own game and was soon barred from one casino after another. In 1981, when even the biggest casinos refused him play, Cardoza founded Cardoza Publishing, which has sold more than five million books and published close to 100 gaming titles.

Though originally from Brooklyn, New York, where he is occasionally found, Cardoza has used his winnings to pursue a lifestyle of extensive traveling in exotic locales around the world.

In 1994, he established Cardoza Entertainment, a multimedia development and publishing house, to produce interactive gambling simulations that give players a taste of a real casino with animated and responsive dealers, and the full scale of bets at the correct odds. The result, *Avery Cardoza's Casino*, featuring 65 gambling variations, became an instant entertainment hit making its way onto USA Today's best-seller's list. It also catapulted Cardoza Entertainment, measured by average sales per title, as the number two seller of games in the entire industry for the first six months of 1997, ahead of such giants as Dreamworks, Microsoft, and others. Their second title, *Avery Cardoza's 100 Slots*, was a simulated slots palace with 101 machines, and became another best-seller.

Avery Cardoza's new online gambling lifestyle magazine is free to view on the web at www.cardozacity.com.

HOW TO PLAY
WINNING
POKER

AVERY CARDOZA

CARDOZA PUBLISHING

FREE ONLINE GAMBLING MAGAZINE
www.cardozacity.com

Check out Cardoza Publishing's new super mega-site gambling magazine. This content-rich publication is targeted to *you* and loaded with articles, columns, how-to information, and much more on the world of gambling.
come visit us now! • www.cardozacity.com

Cardoza Publishing is the foremost gaming and gambling publisher in the world with a library of more than 100 up-to-date and easy-to-read books and strategies. These authoritative works are written by the top experts in their fields. With more than 6,500,000 books in print, they represent the best-selling and most popular gaming books anywhere.

Fourth Edition

Copyright©1987, 1993, 1999, 2003 by Avery Cardoza
-All Rights Reserved-

Library of Congress Catalog Card No: 2003100563
ISBN: 1-58042-098-2

Write for your free full color catalogue of gambling books, advanced strategies, and computer strategies.

CARDOZA PUBLISHING
PO Box 1500 Cooper Station, New York, NY 10276
Phone 1-800-577-WINS
E-Mail: cardozapub@aol.com
www.cardozapub.com

TABLE OF CONTENTS

1. INTRODUCTION

Poker is the greatest and most exciting gambling game. It's an American tradition, where rich and poor, men and women of all classes gather around a table and vie for stakes ranging from mere pennies to thousands of dollars. No other game provides both the challenges of skill, luck, and psychology and the drama of the bluff in such a fascinating weave.

In this book, I'll show you how to conquer these challenges and be a winner at poker! I cover the major poker variations: draw poker (jacks or better, anything opens, and lowball), seven-card stud (high, low, and high-low), hold 'em, and Omaha high-low 8 or better. I will show you the basics of play for each of these games. We'll then discuss the differences between casino and private games and go into all the fundamentals of poker: the jargon, the rules of the games, the player's options, the ranks of hands for high, low, and wild-card poker, how to bet, how to play, and everything else you need to make you an informed player.

In addition to my sections on the basics of play at each of the games, I've also included chapters on winning concepts, bluffing, and general strategies. You'll learn how to recognize lock, strong, marginal, and weak hands, and how to play these cards, how to play position at the table, how to use pot odds to determine the soundness of a bet, how to read your opponents' playing styles and cash in on the information they give you, how to play against opponents who bluff a lot or rarely bluff or are loose or tight players, and much, much more. By adjusting your play accordingly, you'll have a big edge on your opponents.

It's all here in this book. Read on so you can get out there and win!

2. HISTORY

Poker is a truly great gambling game whose popularity seems to grow with time. It flourishes in private homes and clubs throughout the United States and Canada, and it has devotees around the world as well. For many players, the Friday night poker game has been an uninterrupted ritual for years.

The first seeds of poker drifted across the oceans from the European and Asian continents in the early 1800s. They found cultivation around the burgeoning Mississippi River port of New Orleans. The Louisiana Purchase of 1803 opened up a wild and new frontier, and soon thereafter, poker began to capture the gambling spirits and imagination of the new settlers.

The original American poker game used only a 20-card deck of four suits: spades, diamonds, clubs and hearts. The deck contained four each of aces, kings, queens, jacks and 10s, one ordinal per suit. This early form did not yet recognize straights and flushes. Card games from Persia (As Nas or As), France (Poque) and Germany (Pochen or Poch) are credited with being the forerunners of poker.

HOW TO PLAY WINNING POKER

By the 1840's, the full 52-card deck had been adopted, with the four suits now represented in card values of aces (high) through deuces (low). Straights and flushes made their way into the game by the late 1850's, establishing poker in its more or less modern day form.

3. THE BASICS OF POKER

OBJECT OF THE GAME

The player's object in poker is to win the money in the **pot**—the accumulation of bets and antes gathered in the center of the table. You can win in two ways. The first way is to have the highest ranking hand at the **showdown**—the final act in poker, where all active players' hands are revealed to see who has the best one. The second way is to be the last one in when all other players have dropped out of play. In these instances, there is no showdown and the remaining player automatically wins the pot.

PARTICIPANTS

Poker can be played with as few as two players to as many as the 52-card deck can support, usually around eight or nine players. One version of poker, hold 'em, can theoretically support as many as twenty players, though games with more than eleven players are rarely seen in any poker variation.

In a private game, one of the players is designated as the **dealer**—the person who shuffles and deals the cards to the players. The dealer position changes with each hand, rotating around the table in a clockwise direction, with each player having a chance to deal. The dealer is still an active player in a private game and enjoys no advantage other than any positional edge he may have for the particular game played.

In casino poker, the dealer is a house employee and non-player. In addition to shuffling and dealing the cards, the house dealer is responsible for supervising and generally running the game. He ensures that all betting is in order and that the proper procedures of play are followed.

In casino variations where the dealer enjoys a positional advantage, such as hold 'em, lowball, Omaha, and draw poker, a **button** is utilized to designate the imaginary dealer's position. The button rotates around the table, one spot at a time, in clockwise fashion, so that, as in the private game, each player in turn has a chance to enjoy the advantages of acting last.

Each player in poker plays by himself and for himself alone against all other players. Collusion or partnership play are both illegal and are considered cheating.

THE DECK OF CARDS

Poker is played with a standard 52-card deck containing four suits of thirteen cards each: clubs, diamonds, spades and hearts. The cards are valued in descending order, with the ace being the most powerful. It's followed by the king, queen, jack, 10, 9, 8, 7, 6, 5, 4, 3, and, finally, the **deuce** or 2, which is the lowest ranked card. The king, queen and the jack are known as **picture cards** or **face cards**.

The Four Suits

The four suits in poker have no basic value in the determination of winning hands. As you shall see, it is not the value of the individual cards that reign supreme in poker, but the *combination of cards* which determine the value of a player's hand.

CARD ABBREVIATIONS

I will refer to the cards by the following commonly used symbols: ace (A), king (K), queen (Q), jack (J), and all others directly by their numerical value. Thus, the three will be indicated by (3), nine by (9), and the ten by (10).

RANK OF HANDS: HIGH POKER

Poker is generally played as high poker. Listed here are the relative rankings of hands in descending order, from best to worst. (Note that all poker hands eventually consist of five cards, regardless of the variation played.)

HOW TO PLAY WINNING POKER

ROYAL FLUSH

A hand of A K Q J 10, all of the same suit, is called a **royal flush**. For example, A♠ K♠ Q♠ J♠ 10♠ is a royal flush. The odds of being dealt a royal flush in a five-card poker game are 1 in 649,740.

The royal flush is the most powerful hand in poker, and a player may never see it in a lifetime of play. In the extremely unlikely event that two players hold royal flushes, the hand is a tie and the pot is split.

Royal Flush

STRAIGHT FLUSH

Five other cards of the same suit in numerical sequence, such as Q♦ J♦ 10♦ 9♦ 8♦, is called a **straight flush**. That particular example is called a queen-high straight flush, since the queen is the highest ranking card. The straight flush is the second most powerful hand in poker.

Straight Flush

THE BASICS OF POKER

When two straight flushes are in competition for the pot, the straight flush with the highest ranking card wins. Thus, for example, a queen-high straight flush beats out a 10-high straight flush. If two players hold equivalently ranked straight flushes, such as 9♣ 8♣ 7♣ 6♣ 5♣ and 9♥ 8♥ 7♥ 6♥ 5♥, then the hand is a tie and the pot is split. Suits have no dominance over one another in poker.

The ace can be used as either the highest card in the straight flush (an ace-high hand being a royal flush) or the lowest card, as in A♦ 2♦ 3♦ 4♦ 5♦, to be valid. The hand of Q♣ K♣ A♣ 2♣ 3♣ is not a straight flush. It's simply a flush.

FOUR-OF-A-KIND

A hand of four cards of identical rank, such as the hand J J J J 3, is called a **four-of-a-kind**, and is almost a sure win in straight poker (poker without a wild card). The odd card in the above example, the 3, is irrelevant and has no bearing on the rank of the hand. When two players hold a four-of-a-kind, the higher ranking four-of-a-kind will win the hand. For example, J J J J 3 beats out 7 7 7 7 A.

Four-of-a-Kind

FULL HOUSE

A **full house** consists of three cards of identical rank along with two cards of an identical but different rank. 3 3 3 A A and 5 5 5 7 7 are two examples of full houses.

Full House

When two players hold full houses, it is the hand holding the higher ranking three-of-a-kind that wins the pot. In the above example, the latter hand, 5 5 5 7 7, is the higher ranking full house.

FLUSH

Any five cards of the same suit constitutes a **flush**. A hand of A♠ K♠ 7♠ 3♠ 2♠ is called an ace-high flush in spades and Q♥ 10♥ 7♥ 5♥ 3♥ is a queen-high flush in hearts. When two or more players hold flushes, the flush with the highest ranking card wins the pot. In the above example, the ace-high flush holds the higher ranking card, the ace. It's therefore the stronger hand.

Flush

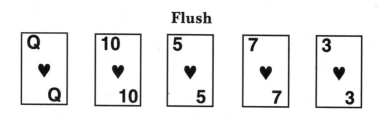

If the highest ranking cards in competing flushes are of equivalent rank, the next highest cards decide the winner. If they too are tied, then the next cards, and so on, down to the fifth card if need be. For example, in the two flushes K♦ Q♦ 9♦ 7♦ 6♦ and K♥ Q♥ J♥ 5♥ 2♥, the heart flush is the stronger flush, since its third highest ranking card, the jack, is higher ranking than the 9, the diamond flush's third highest ranking card.

When all five cards of competing flushes are identical, the hand is a tie, and the winners split the pot. Suits are irrelevant in determining a higher ranking flush.

STRAIGHT

A hand of five non-suited cards in sequential order, such as 10 9 8 7 6, is called a **straight**. When straights contain an ace, the ace must serve as either the highest card in the run—such as the ace-high straight A K Q J 10—or the lowest card—as in the 5-high straight 5 4 3 2 A. The hand Q K A 2 3 is not a straight. It's merely an ace-high hand. Even a lowly pair beats it.

Straight

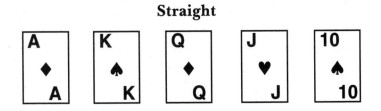

When two or more straights are in competition,

the straight with the highest ranking card takes the pot. A 9-high straight beats out a 7-high straight. When two straights are of equal value, the hand is a tie and the pot is split.

THREE-OF-A-KIND

A hand of three matched cards of identical value, along with two odd cards (unmatched) is called a **three-of-a-kind**. 7 7 7 Q 2 is called "three sevens" or "trip 7s." When two players hold three-of-a-kind, the player with the higher ranking triplets takes the pot. The jacks in J J J 3 4 beat out the trip 8 hand of 8 8 8 Q 5.

Three-of-a-Kind

TWO PAIR

A hand with two sets of equivalently valued or "paired" cards, along with an unmatched card, is called two pair. 10 10 8 8 5 is a two-paired hand called "tens up" or "tens over eights," since the tens are the higher ranking pair. Similarly, A A 3 3 J is called "aces up" or "aces over threes."

Two Pair

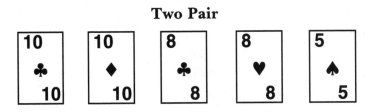

If more than one player holds a two pair hand, the winner would be the player holding the higher ranked of the two paired hand. J J 7 7 K beats out 10 10 9 9 A. When the higher ranking pairs are identical, the next paired cards determine the winner. 8 8 4 4 10 loses to 8 8 5 5 9. When both pairs are evenly matched, the higher ranking fifth card—the odd card—determines the victor. If all cards are equally ranked, such as 5 5 3 3 2 and 5 5 3 3 2, then the hand is a tie and the pot is split.

ONE PAIR

A hand with one set of identically valued cards, along with three unmatched cards is called a pair. The hand 2 2 8 4 A is called "a pair of twos." Pairs are ranked in order of value from aces, the highest, down to the deuces, the lowest. Thus, a pair of aces beats a pair of kings, and a pair of nines wins over a pair of sixes.

One Pair

HOW TO PLAY WINNING POKER

When two players hold equally paired hands, the highest odd card decides the winner. 8 8 Q 7 3 triumphs over 8 8 J 9 7. If the highest unmatched cards are also equivalently valued, then the next highest cards are compared, and then the last cards if necessary. J J 10 9 8 beats J J 10 9 7. If all cards are identical, the hand is a tie and the pot is split.

HIGH CARD

A hand containing five unmatched cards—that is, lacking any of the above combinations: a pair, two pairs, three-of-a-kind, straights, flushes, full houses, four-of-a-kind, straight flushes or royal flushes—is valued by its highest ranking card. For example, the hand A 10 9 8 7 is considered an "ace-high" hand. It beats the lesser "king-high" hand of K Q J 4 3.

When the highest ranking cards are identical, the hand with the next highest card wins. If those too are equivalent, then the next two highest are compared and so on, through the fifth card. The hand K Q 7 5 2 beats K Q 7 4 3. If all cards are identical, the hand is a draw, and the pot is split.

King-High Hand

There are a total of 2,598,960 five-card combinations possible with a 52-card deck. The following chart illustrates the chances of being dealt each type of hand.

Probabilities of Five-Card Poker Hands		
Hand	**Number**	**Approximate Odds**
Royal Flush	4	649,740 to 1
Straight Flush	36	72,192 to 1
Four-of-a-Kind*	624	4,164 to 1
Full House	3,744	693 to 1
Flush	5,108	508 to 1
Straight	10,200	254 to 1
Three-of-a-Kind	54,912	46 to 1
Two Pair	123,552	20 to 1
One Pair	1,098,240	1.37 to 1
No Hand	1,302,540	1 to 1

*Though there are only 13 four-of-a-kind combinations, this calculation takes into account the total number of possibilities when the fifth card is figured in to make a five-card hand.

WILD CARDS

In some poker games, players will designate certain cards as **wild cards**. These are cards which can take on any value and suit at the holder's discretion—they can even be a duplicate of a card already held. Sometimes the "53rd" and "54th" cards of the deck, the jokers, are used as wilds. Players might also designate the deuces or the one-eyed jacks as wild cards. Any card can be considered wild with the consent of all players.

HOW TO PLAY WINNING POKER

If the deuces were used as wild cards, for example, the hand 6 5 3 2 2 could be a straight by designating one deuce as a 7 and the other as a 4. At the showdown, the holder of this hand would represent a 7-high straight as his best total.

RANK OF HANDS: WILD CARD POKER

The only difference in the ranking of hands in wild card poker from the ranking in high poker is that five-of-a-kind in wild poker is the highest ranking hand. Otherwise, all other rankings, from the royal flush down to the high card, follow the same relative scale.

Here are the relative rankings of hands, from highest to lowest, in wild card poker.

Ranks of Hands · Wild Card Poker

Five-of-a-Kind
Royal Flush
Straight Flush
Four-of-a-Kind
Full House
Flush
Straight
Three-of-a-Kind
Two Pairs
One Pair
High Card

THE BASICS OF POKER

RANK OF HANDS: LOW POKER

In low poker, the ranking of hands is the opposite to that of high poker, with the lowest hand being the most powerful. The ace is considered the lowest and therefore most powerful card. The hand 5 4 3 2 A is the best low total possible. (See the section on Lowball for further discussion of low poker rankings.)

MONEY AND CHIPS

Chips are the standard and accepted currency for casino and private poker games, though cash is sometimes used as well. Players prefer the use of chips for betting purposes as the handling of money at the tables is cumbersome and can slow a game down. There's something impersonal and distant about chips, and using them removes players from the reality of losing actual money when they lose.

In casino poker, the standard denominations of chips are $1, $5, $25, and $100. In big money games, you can sometimes find $1,000 and $5000 chips. In games with 25¢ and 50¢ antes, regular quarters and half dollars are also used. Though some casinos use their own color code, the typical color scheme of poker chips is : $1 – blue, $5 – red, $25 – green, and $100 – black.

To receive chips in a casino game, give the dealer cash, and he'll give you back the equivalent value in chips. This exchange of cash for chips is called a **buy-in**. Dealers will accept only cash or chips, so if you have traveler's checks, credit cards, or other forms of money, you need to exchange these for cash at the area marked **Casino Cashier**. Then, with cash in hand, you can buy chips at the poker table.

In private games, players generally use chips, though sometimes the game will be cash only. When chips are used, one player acts as the **bank** or **banker**. He converts players' cash buy-ins to equivalent values in chips. The most common denominations of chips used in private games are one unit, five units, ten units, and twenty-five units. A unit can equal a penny, a dollar, or whatever value is agreed upon and set by the players.

One unit chips are generally white, five units are red, ten units are blue, and twenty-five units are yellow, though any equivalencies or colors may be used.

PRELIMINARIES OF PLAY

The dealer is responsible for shuffling the cards after each round of play so that they are mixed well and in random order. The deck is then offered to a player, usually on the dealer's right, for the **cut**. This player initiates the cut by removing the top part of the deck and placing it to one side, face down. The dealer completes the cut by placing the former lower portion of the deck on top of the former upper section, thereby effecting the cut, and making the deck of cards whole again.

THE BASICS OF POKER

To be valid, a cut must go deeper than the top five cards of the deck and may not go further in than the last five. This rule helps prevent players who had inadvertently (or otherwise) seen the top or bottom cards from using the cut to undue advantage. A cut of any number of cards between these two extremes is valid and perfectly acceptable.

The game is ready to begin.

ANTES

An **ante**, also known as a **sweetener**, is a uniform bet placed into the pot by players before the cards are dealt. The size of the ante is prearranged by the players, or in a casino is set by the house. All players are required to pay the ante.

The ante is used in a majority of private poker games and virtually all casino games. It's a way to "sweeten the pie" and create more action in the game. The ante creates an immediate pot, which sharp players, under the right circumstances, may go after right from the start. A player will bet forcefully in first round play hoping to force opposing players out of the pot. If he succeeds, he'll win the pot and the antes in it immediately, by process of elimination. This move is called **stealing the ante**.

THE PLAY OF THE GAME

After the dealer shuffles the cards and offers the cut, the deal is ready to begin. If the game requires an ante, the dealer may announce **"ante-up,"** a call for all players to place their antes into the pot. The center of the table is used as the area for the pot, and that is where all antes and bets should be placed.

The dealer begins dealing to the player on his immediate left. He deals cards one at a time in a clockwise rotation, until each player has received the requisite number of cards for the poker variation being played. In casino games, where a rotating **button** is used to mark the dealer's position, the deal begins with the player to the left of the button. It continues around in the same fashion as in private games.

Like the dealing of the cards, play always proceeds in clockwise fashion. The first round begins with either the player sitting to the immediate left of the dealer, or, in some of the stud games, with either the high or low card opening play. Play continues around the table, until each player in turn has acted.

In later rounds, the first player to act will vary depending on the poker variation being played. In the stud games, the strongest ranking open cards will open betting. In the draw games, either the first active player to the left of the dealer will open betting, or the last player to have raised or opened in the previous round will initiate play.

We'll cover the particulars of play under the sections on the games themselves. You'll then see how

THE BASICS OF POKER

the betting works for the different variations.

THE PLAYER'S OPTIONS
Except for the times when a bet is mandatory—as is usually the case in the initial round of play—the first player to act in a betting round has three options:

1. He can place a **bet**, which means he'll wager money and place it into the pot.

2. He can **check** or **pass**, which means he'll make no bet at all and will just pass play on to the next player, while still remaining an active player.

3. He can **fold** or **go out**, which means he'll throw away his cards and forfeit future play during the current deal.

Once a bet is placed, however, a player no longer has the option of checking his turn. To remain an active player, he must either **call the bet** or **see the bet** (place an amount of money into the pot equal to the bet) or **raise** or **call and raise** (call the bet and make an additional bet on top of the bet called). If a player doesn't want to bet, then he must fold and go out of play. Each succeeding player, in turn, is faced with the same options: calling, folding, or raising.

To continue playing for the pot, a player must call the original bet and any raises that were made. A player may choose to fold his cards if he doesn't want to call the bets and raises that preceded him.

When play swings around again to the original bettor, he must call any previous raises to continue as an active player, as must any subsequent players who have raises due. A player who doesn't wish to call the raises must fold. (If the raise limit hasn't been reached, a player may also raise again.)

The number of raises permitted varies from game to game. Generally, though, casino games are limited to either three or five total raises in one round, except when just two players remain. This situation is called **head to head** play, when unlimited raising is allowed. Most private games allow unlimited raising at all times. A player may not, however, raise his own bet. He may raise only another player's bet or raise.

Play continues until the last bet or raise is called by all active players, and no more bets or raises are due from any player. The betting round is now completed and over. One important rule of poker etiquette is that players may check, bet, raise, or fold during their proper turns only. This rule must always be respected by all players.

Some games use a **blind**–a mandatory bet that is made by the first player to act in the opening round of play. This player, called the **blind bettor**, must make the blind bet regardless of the hand he or she holds. The blind is a forced bet, and it forces immediate action in a poker game. When there are two blinds, as is the case in many games, then the next player in turn will be forced to make a blind bet as well. These two bettors are known as the small blind and the big blind. The **small blind**, the first player to make the forced bet, is usually required to bet half the minimum bet, while **the big blind** is required to bet the full minimum. In a $5-$10 game, for example, the small blind would bet $5, and the big blind would bet $10.

Players cannot check after a blind bet is made. They must either call the blind, raise, or fold. Otherwise, play proceeds the same as it does in games which don't use a blind. The amount of a blind bet varies, but it is usually less than or equal to the minimum bet.

Check and raise, a player's raising of a bet afterpreviously checking in a round, is usually not allowed in private games, but many casino games permit it. If you're interested in this play, ask if check and raise is allowed before you sit down to play in a game.

BETTING LIMITS (LIMIT POKER)

Betting in poker is generally structured in a two-tiered fashion. The lower level of betting occurs before the draw in the draw poker variations or in the early rounds of the stud games. The upper level occurs after the draw in the draw poker games and in the later rounds in the stud variations. Some commonly used betting structures are $1-$2, $1-$3, $5-$10, and $15-$30, though other limits are found as well.

In a $5-$10 limit game, when the lower limit of betting is in effect, all bets and raises must be in $5 increments. When the upper range is in effect, all bets and raises must be in $10 increments. We'll discuss when the lower and upper ranges of betting are in play for each of the games during the sections covering the individual poker variations.

The betting limits of casino games are generally posted above the table. You can also learn them by asking the dealer or one of the players. The betting limits of private games are prearranged and agreed upon by the players before playing.

TABLE STAKES

Table stakes is a rule in casino poker and almost all private games. It states that a player's bet or call of a bet may not exceed the amount of money he has on the table in front of him. For example, if the bet due from a player is $25, and he has only $10 remaining on the table, this player is considered **tapped-out**. He may call the bet only to the tune of $10. He is not allowed to withdraw money from his wallet, borrow from others, or receive credit during a deal. Those actions are permissible only before the cards are dealt.

In the above example, the remaining $15 and all

future monies bet during this hand would be seg-regated into a separate pot, called a **side pot**. The tapped-out player can still receive cards until the showdown and play for the original pot, but he can no longer take part in the betting, and has no in-terest in the side pot. The other players, however, can continue to bet and wager against each other for the side pot as well.

Should the tapped-out player have the best hand at the showdown, he would receive only the money in the original pot. The side pot is won by the player having the best hand among the remaining play-ers. Should one of the other players hold the over-all best hand, that player wins both the original and the side pot.

If only one other bettor remains when a player taps out, then there is no more betting. Cards are sim-ply played out until the showdown. In the above example, the opposing player would have $15 of his $25 bet returned to him, since only $10 of his bet can be called. At the showdown, the best hand would win the existing pot.

POT LIMIT AND NO LIMIT

Poker is sometimes played as pot limit or no limit. These are betting structures often used in high stakes poker games. **Pot limit** games allow players to bet any amount up to the current size of the pot but no more. For example, if the pot holds $75, the largest allowable bet is $75. If a player then bets pot limit and places $75 more into the pot, the pot would now contain $150. The betting limit is now set at a maximum of $150.

No limit poker is even a wilder version. It states that a player's maximum bet is limited only by the table stakes rule. The World Series of Poker played at the Horseshoe Casino in Las Vegas every year plays no limit style of hold 'em poker with a $10,000 buy-in.

Pot limit and no limit poker are too vicious for the average player (unless comfortable maximum betting ranges are set by the players) and should not be considered by anyone but top level players with big purses. In this book, we'll assume just the limit variety of poker, the game almost universally played by most players in private and casino games.

SAMPLE ROUND OF BETTING

For illustrative purposes, let's follow the play in the first betting round of a private game of draw poker: anything opens. This game is played without a blind (as is jacks or better), and the first player to act may check or bet as desired. In the other games we'll discuss—hold 'em, draw poker: lowball, and the seven-card stud variations—the opening player has no such luxury. He must either make the mandatory opening bet or fold (when allowed). In these games, checking is not allowed in first round play. We'll look at the particular rules of play for each game in the individual games sections, and there

I'll show which player is the first to act in a betting round and whether that player must make a mandatory opening bet.

Let's pick up the action now and see how the betting works. The eight players have agreed to play with a $1 ante, so the pot holds $8 before any of the cards are dealt. The participants are, in order, clockwise from the dealer: Julian, Eddie-boy, Vicenzo, Fay, Donto, Flavian, Uncle J. and Big Phil (the current dealer).

They are playing **dealer's choice**, a rule which allows each successive dealer to choose the variation played during his deal. In casino poker games, dealer's choice is not played, and players are limited to playing the variations designated for their table. If a player wishes to play a different variation, he must switch to a table offering the game he desires.

Big Phil is the current dealer, and he has chosen draw poker: anything opens as the game he wants to deal. The player sitting to the immediate left of the dealer goes first in draw poker. After the cards are dealt, all players await Julian's decision.

Julian raps on the table with his knuckles. This is a nonverbal signal used in poker to indicate that a player is checking. He may also indicate checking by saying "Check" or "Pass" or some such communication. Eddie-boy and Vicenzo, in turn, check as well. Play passes on to Fay, the next player.

Fay announces, "I'll bet $5," and throws a $5 chip into the pot. Now that a bet is placed, no player can check and remain in the game.

Donto, sitting at Fay's left, decides his hand isn't worth $5. He flips his cards face down toward the dealer. Donto is no longer a participant in the pot, and he forfeits his $1 ante. He must wait until the next deal to resume play.

Flavian draws a big puff out of his cigar. "Cuban," he claims, and throws $10 into the pot, calling Fay's $5 bet and raising it $5 more. He announces, "$10 to you, Uncle J."

Raises, like bets, are made by the physical placement of chips in the pot area. It is often the custom in a private game to announce them as well. Raising may be indicated by saying, "I'll raise you" or "I'll call that bet and raise," or any such communication that clearly indicates that a raise is being made.

Uncle J. must be daunted by either the $10 he's due or the cigar, and he folds. Big Phil, the dealer for this round of play, calls the $5 bet and the $5 raise, and re-raises $5 more. He places $15 into the pot.

Flavian's cigar whirls across his mouth like a brigate cannon searching out new targets, and sends the long overdue ashes crashing against the dizzying colors of his Hawaiian short-sleeved shirt. One ash, still hot, works its way into a palm tree, and then fades away in lasting glory.

Play now returns to Julian, who had checked earlier. To stay in the hand, he must call $15 worth of bets—one $5 bet plus two $5 raises. He throws his cards in without hesitation, and is followed by Eddie-boy, who does the same. Vicenzo, who had also checked, bets the $15. He may not raise, since this private game does not allow check-and-raise. If check-and-raise were permitted, he would be allowed to raise $5 more. Since this is the first round of betting, all bets and raises are in $5 increments. $10 bets and raises are not allowed in this round.

Fay plays next, and she must call the two $5 raises of her original bet to stay in. She might have called just one raise, but with two raises facing her and Flavian's cigar bent at a mean angle, she decides her hand is not worth $10 more. She folds. She's out her earlier $5 bet and $1 ante—that money now belongs to the pot.

Play passes by Donto, since he had folded earlier, and proceeds to Flavian, the first raiser, and his cigar. Since his raise had been upped $5 by Big Phil, he must call that re-raise to play. The cigar rotates slowly as Flavian weighs the possibility of raising again, and then pointedly stops, aimed dead ahead at the middle of Big Phil's forehead. Another second passes, drawn out by a long puff, and then Flavian flips a $5 chip into the pot, calling Big Phil's raise.

The only active players remaining are, in order, Big Phil, Vicenzo, and Flavian. Big Phil cannot raise again. He was the last player to raise, and a player cannot raise his own bet. Since all bets and raises have been called by the remaining players, the betting round is over.

THE SHOWDOWN

Following the conclusion of all betting in the final betting round, if two or more players remain, the **showdown** occurs. The showdown is the final act in a poker game where remaining players reveal their hands to determine the winner of the pot.

The player whose last bet or raise was called is the first to turn over his cards and reveal his hand. If his hand proves to be the best, he wins the pot and collects all the money in it. However, any player who claims a superior hand must show it. Players holding losing hands at the showdown may concede the pot without showing their cards.

The player with the best hand at the showdown wins all the money in the pot. In the event of a tie, or when there are two winners—as may be the case in high-low—the pot is split evenly among the winners. If only one player remains after the final betting round, or at any point during the game, there is no showdown. The lone remaining player automatically wins the pot.

THE RAKE

The biggest difference between casino poker and private poker games is that in the casino games the house gets a cut of the action, called a **rake**, for its services. The rake varies from casino to casino. It's usually proportionately higher in lower limit games.

Don't play in a game where the rake is greater than five percent of the total bet made. It's too much of an overhead. Find a more reasonable game, where your winnings won't dwindle away to nothing because of weighty house cuts. Always ask how much the house rake is before you sit down to play.

THE RULES OF THE TABLE

Though poker is basically the same game played anywhere, at home or in the casino, rules can vary from game to game. Make sure that you're clear about the particulars of play before sitting down at a new poker game. The most important questions to ask are:

1. What are the betting limits?
2. Is "check-and-raise" allowed?
3. Are antes or blinds used, and if so, how much are they?
4. What is the maximum number of raises allowed?

HOW TO PLAY WINNING POKER

When you're playing a casino game, most of the above information may be posted on a sign above the table, but if it isn't, ask the dealer or a player and find out. In casino games, you should also ask a fifth question: "How much is the rake?"

4. DRAW POKER

JACKS OR BETTER

Also called **jackpots, draw poker - jacks or better** is a **closed poker** variation, where all cards are dealt face down (closed) and known only by the holder of that hand. It is played with two betting rounds. The first betting round occurs before the **draw**, when players have an opportunity to exchange up to three unwanted cards for new ones. In some games, players are allowed to draw four cards if their remaining card is an ace, and in casino draw poker, players may exchange up to five unwanted cards for new ones.

The second round of betting occurs after the draw. At the showdown, the highest hand wins the pot. If all other players have folded, the last remaining player is the winner.

THE PLAY OF THE GAME

Both the casino and private versions of jacks or better require antes. These must be placed into the pot before the cards are dealt. Antes usually range from 10% of the maximum bet (normal size) to 20%

(considered a high ante). In a $5-$10 game, a $1 or $2 ante would be the most common found.

Each player is dealt five face-down cards. The deal begins with the player to the immediate left of the dealer receiving the first card and continues clockwise, one card at a time, until all players have received their five cards. The first round of betting begins at this point, with the first player to have received cards, the one on the dealer's left, making the first play.

To open betting in jacks or better, a player must have a hand with a minimum ranking of a pair of jacks. For example, a pair of queens, three deuces or a straight are hands that could open betting, while a pair of 7s or an ace-high hand could not. A player holding jacks or better does not have to open betting, however. He may check his turn.

The first player to act must check if he cannot open betting or chooses not to open. The next player, in turn, must also check if he doesn't hold the requisite opening cards. Players continue checking until an **opener**, the opening bet with a hand of jacks or better, is made.

Once an opening bet is placed, subsequent players, in order, may call, fold or raise the opener. Checking is no longer permitted. A bet has been made and players must call that bet to play for the pot. Play continues around the table in clockwise fashion until all bets and raises have been called. If all players check on the opening round of play, the hand is said to be **passed out**. The cards are collected and shuffled, and the next player in turn gets the dealer's position. New antes will be required of all players. These are added to the antes already in the pot.

The draw occurs after the first betting round is completed. Each remaining player, beginning with the first active player to the dealer's left, can discard up to three cards (or five when allowed). The cards should be tossed face-down toward the dealer, who will issue an equivalent number of new cards from the unused portion of the deck. Players should draw in turn, waiting for the previous player to receive his new cards before making their own discards. The dealer draws last, if he is still in the pot.

Discards should be announced, so that all players are aware of the number of cards drawn. Players who do not draw any cards are said to stand **pat**. You can indicate your choice to stand pat verbally or by knocking on the table with your hand.

The second round of betting follows the draw. It is begun by either the opener or the last raiser if there were any raises during the round. If no raises occurred, and the opener has folded, the first active player to the dealer's left opens the betting. This player may check or bet as desired. Each succeeding player has the option of checking or betting, but once a bet is placed, active players must call that bet, raise, or go out.

The showdown occurs after this betting round is completed. At this time, the player whose last bet or raise was called (as opposed to players calling those bets) turns over his cards first. Any opponent who claims a superior hand must turn over his cards for verification. Players holding inferior hands may go out without revealing their cards. The best hand wins the pot and gets to rake in the chips.

Let's return to our original crew and see how the betting works in a $5-$10 limit game of jacks or better. They're playing with a $2 ante, a high ante for this type of betting, and one which encourages aggressive early betting to "steal the antes." The pot holds $16 to start (eight players times $2).

These are the cards they hold after the deal:

Julian	K	10	7	3	2
Eddie-boy	8	8	10	4	2
Vicenzo	A	A	J	10	8
Fay	6	6	A	4	3
Donto	A	J	7	6	3
Flavian	K	10	9	8	7
Uncle J.	J	J	5	4	2
Big Phil	5	5	5	8	7

Julian is on the dealer's immediate left, so he opens play. Not having a hand of jacks or better, Julian checks, as does Eddie-boy, who holds only a pair of 8s. Vicenzo can open, and he does, flipping a $5 chip into the pot. Fay has nothing worth betting on, and she folds.

Donto is excited enough by his ace-high hand to call the bet, but it's a poor play. He's a big underdog with those cards and has little chance of winning.

Flavian's cigar is blowing smoke like a train coming down the tracks. With two players in the action and a large ante, the $25 in the pot gives him good pot odds to go for his straight (26-5, greater than the approximately 4-1 odds he needs to make the play justifiable) and he calls the $5 bet as well.

Uncle J. knows that the opener, Vicenzo, holds jacks or better, and he figures that Vicenzo probably has at least kings or aces to have opened in such an early position. With two other players in the game, he folds his pair of jacks. He knows they're of little value.

Big Phil tosses $10 into the pot, calling the $5 opener and bumping that bet $5 more. His three fives are strong cards. If too many players are allowed to draw out against them, they could get beat.

Julian and Eddie-boy see that their free ride is over and fold in turn. Neither sees his cards being worth a $5 bet, let alone a $5 raise on top. Vicenzo calls the raise and flips his $5 into the pot. Donto finally folds, poorer by his earlier $5 call. Flavian is playing for the draw and calls the $5 raise.

The raise has now been called by all active players, and the first betting round is over. On this first round of betting, before the draw, all bets and raises are in the lower tier of the $5-$10 game, and are therefore in $5 increments. After the draw, all bets will be in the upper tier, or in $10 increments.

Three players remain for the draw: Vicenzo, Flavian, and Big Phil. Vicenzo throws his discards toward the dealer and draws three cards to his aces. Flavian calls for one card. After he receives his draw, Big Phil takes one card as well. Though Big Phil theoretically has better chances of improving his hand with a two-card draw, his one-card draw is a clever play, since opponents must figure him for two pair. Meanwhile, he's sitting pretty with his three 5s, a favorite against his two opponents.

Here's how the hands look after the draw:

Vicenzo	A	A	9	9	2
Flavian	10	9	8	7	4
Big Phil	5	5	5	K	6

The opener, Vicenzo, acts first and bets $10. His aces over 9s is a strong hand, and he figures it's a stronger hand than Big Phil's probable two pair. Flavian's train has slowed down, and he folds. The

4 that he drew fell a little short of his needs. There's not much he can do with a 10-high hand.

Big Phil raises the bet to $20 (a $10 raise) and Vicenzo calls the bet. Since Vicenzo called Big Phil's raise, Big Phil must show his cards first. He turns over his trip 5s. Vicenzo sees that he is beat, and, mumbling something about his boss, throws his cards face down and concedes the pot.

Big Phil is the winner. He collects all the chips in the pot, giving them a new home in his private stack. A new deal is ready to begin.

STRATEGY FOR JACKS OR BETTER

As with all the other poker variations, the single most important strategy in jacks or better is to start out with cards which have good winning possibilities. The opening requirement of jacks or better tells you right off that any pair you hold which is less than the minimum opening hand of jacks is automatically a big underdog. For example, if an opponent opens the betting, what chances do your pair of 8s have against this opener? You know that he has jacks or better.

Position is also an important consideration in jackpots. The relative position a player has in the order of betting affects the types of hands that he should play and how he should bet those hands. For example, if a player opens betting with a pair of jacks or queens in an early position, he's in a bad situation if his opener gets raised by several players. You have to figure the raisers for at least kings or aces, possibly better, and against a lowly pair of jacks, nobody is scared. The jacks are underdogs and must be folded.

Let's examine the minimum requirements for correct play in jacks or better.

Jacks or Better · Minimum Opening Cards	
First Four Positions (Early):	Kings or Better
Second Two Positions (Middle):	Queens or Better
Last Two Positions (Late):	Jacks or Better

In late position, when no openers have yet been made, the pair of jacks becomes a stronger hand. The jacks are in a good leveraged position, and an opening bet may be able to force other players out of the pot, effectively stealing the antes. If only one or two players call the opener, the jacks are in a decent enough position going into the draw to improve to a winner.

Once someone has opened the betting, players holding jacks or queens should call only if two players or fewer are in the pot and no raises have been made. Otherwise, you should fold jacks and queens. Their winning chances rapidly diminish as the number of active players increases.

Four-card straights and flushes have good potential. You should play them to the draw, but only if the pot odds justify calling the bet. (See Winning Concept #6 in Chapter 8.) Do not raise with these hands, however. At this stage they're speculative and hold no value. Should the draw fill these cards into a straight or flush, then you've got the goods to be raising and building up the pot.

If you hold kings, aces, and low three-of-a-kind hands, you should not only call the opener but raise as well. These are strong cards. If you don't force out weaker and speculative hands, these inferior hands may bury your favorite with a lucky draw. Against fewer opponents, there's less chance of this occurring. The more players that stay in for the draw, the higher the average winning hand will be, and the greater the opportunity that the kings, aces, and small trips will get beat out by an inferior hand that improves. Raise with these strong cards. Don't make the game cheap for dreamers.

On the other hand, with a high three-of-a-kind, such as trip 10s or higher, don't raise—call! You have a powerful hand which can win without improvement. You want to keep as many players in as possible.

Do not play three card-straights or flushes, or inside straights. An **inside straight** is a four-card straight that has only one way of improving, such as 4 5 7 8. These are nothing hands, and the chances of improving are steeper than a canyon.

PLAYING A SMALL TWO PAIR

Smaller two pair hands, such as 9s over 3s, are deceptive hands in draw poker. You must play them carefully. At first glance, a holding of two small pairs appears to be a strong hand with good winning possibilities. In reality, these cards spell trouble.

While a small two pair may stand tall before the draw, against three players trying to improve as well, that hand in fact becomes an underdog. If you're facing bets and raises before the draw and more bets after it, your small two pair (with 11-1 odds against improving) starts looking even smaller.

Fold two small pairs in early position if the pot is opened ahead of you, or if you're in late position and three or more players are in the pot. In last position, against just one or two players, raise, and try to force them out.

THE DRAW

When you're drawing to a pair, your best odds of improving is to take a three-card draw. Sometimes, however, holding a **kicker**, an extra card to a pair, can be a powerful bluffing tool. Players have to suspect your two-card draw for three-of-a-kind. Occasionally, using the kicker in this fashion can really work to your advantage.

Drawing one card to a three-of-a-kind is a good bluffing strategy as well. Let's say you're playing a $5-$10 game. The first two players check and the third player opens betting with a $5 bet. The next player folds. You're in the next seat holding three 8s, and you raise the opener $5. Players fold in turn around the table. Only the opener calls your bet. He goes first and draws one card. You take one card as well.

After the draw, the opener bets $10, probably holding kings or aces up and figuring you for a lower two pair. You raise $10, banking on the 11-1 odds against his improving. He calls. Then he quietly folds his cards after you turn over your three 8s.

Fold four-flushes and four-straights if they don't improve at the draw.

The dealer has a decisive advantage in draw poker, since he acts last. With marginal hands, he can come in the pot cheaply. He can also fold if the action is too stiff. He's in a great position to bluff, and, being the last to draw, he can make use of his drawing strategy to gain a powerful edge. Due to the dealer's big positional advantage, draw poker is an excellent choice in dealer's choice games.

Play alertly and apply the winning strategies of poker to gain an advantage over your opponents and be a winner at draw poker.

Odds Against Improving Draw Poker Hands

Cards Held	Cards Drawn	Improved To	Approximate Odds Against
One Pair	3	Two Pair	5.3-1
		Three-of-a-Kind	7.8-1
		Full House	97-1
		Four-of-a-Kind	360-1
		Any Improvement	2.5-1
One Pair plus kicker	2	Two Pairs	4.8-1
		Three-of-a-Kind	12-1
		Full House	120-1
		Four-of-a-Kind	1080-1
		Any Improvement	2.8-1
Three-of-a-Kind	2	Full House	15.3-1
		Four-of-a-Kind	22.5-1
		Any Improvement	8.7-1
Four-Card Straight (Open Both Ways)	1	Straight	5-1
Inside Straight	1	Straight	10.8-1
Four-Card Flush	1	Flush	4.2-1
Four-Card Straight Flush (Open Ended)	1	Straight Flush	22.5-1
	1	Straight or Better	2-1
Four-Card Straight Flush (Inside)	1	Straight Flush	46-1
		Straight or Better	3-1

DRAW POKER

DRAW POKER: ANYTHING OPENS

Draw poker: anything opens is played the same as jacks or better except that any hand may open the betting, regardless of strength. For example, a pair of 7s could open betting in anything opens, or even a queen-high hand. Otherwise, the rules and methods of play are identical to jacks or better.

STRATEGY FOR ANYTHING OPENS

The strategies in draw poker: anything opens are virtually the same as in jacks or better. Though any cards can open the betting, don't be fooled into opening or calling bets with anything less than you would play in jackpots. Whether the game requires jacks or better or requires nothing to open betting doesn't change the fact that you'll be dealt just as many good and bad hands in one game as in the other. The same minimum starting hands apply here as in jacks or better.

DRAW POKER: LOWBALL

This interesting variation presents a different twist on poker. The lowest hand is the strongest in **lowball**, or **loball** as it is sometimes spelled, as opposed to the standard high poker game where the highest hand is the best. The ace is still the best card in lowball, but, unlike in high poker, where the ace counts as the highest card held, in this game the ace counts as the lowest card of a hand. The 2 is the next lowest card, and therefore the next best lowball card, and is followed in order by the 3, 4, 5, and so on, up to the king, which is the worst card in lowball.

In lowball, the highest card counts in determining the value of a hand: the lower the highest card, the better the hand. Hands are announced by their two highest cards. For example, the hand 7 6 4 2 A is announced as a "7 6" or "7-high," and 8 4 3 2 A is announced as an "8 4" or "8-high." Of the two above-mentioned hands, the "7 6" is the more powerful lowball hand, since its highest card, the 7, is lower than the 8, the high card of the "8 4" hand.

In instances where the highest values of two hands are equivalent, the next highest cards of the hands are matched up, and the lowest value of these matched cards determines the winner. Thus, the hand 8 6 4 3 2 is a stronger total than 8 7 3 2 A, and 9 6 5 2 A beats out the hand 9 6 5 4 A. When the competing hands are equivalent, such as the holdings 8 5 4 3 A versus 8 5 4 3 A, the hand is considered a tie and the pot is split.

The **wheel** or **bicycle**, 5 4 3 2 A, is the perfect lowball hand. It can never be beat. At best, it can be tied by another wheel. 6 4 3 2 A is the next strongest lowball total, followed in order by 6 5 3 2 A, 6 5 4 2 A, 6 5 4 3 A, and so on.

In lowball, straights and flushes are not relevant and do not count. The wheel, 5 4 3 2 A, is not considered a straight. It's a perfect "5 4." An 8 4 3 2 A, all of hearts is simply an "8 4" hand, not a flush as it would be in high poker.

Any five-card hand containing a pair is a weak hand and can be beat by any five unmatched cards. For example, K Q 7 6 5 is a winner over 2 2 3 4 5. Two pair, three-of-a-kind, full houses, and four-of-a-kind are increasingly worse holdings. The odds of these hands winning are very slim indeed.

The term **smooth** in lowball refers to a relatively good back four cards, such as the hand 9 5 4 3 A, a *smooth* nine. **Rough** suggests a relatively weak back four cards, such as the hand 9 7 6 5 2, a *rough* nine. Lowball is a draw poker variation. As such, it is played similarly to high draw poker, featuring two betting rounds, one before the draw and one after.

THE PLAY OF THE GAME

Lowball is often played with an ante, and that bet should be placed into the pot before the cards are dealt. When no ante is required, a blind bettor is used. Sometimes both a blind bettor and an ante are part of the structure.

After the shuffle and cut, cards are dealt clockwise, one at a time, until all players have received five face down cards. The first player to receive the cards, the one at the immediate left of the button or dealer, is also the first player to act. For purposes of illustration, let's assume a $5-$10 lowball game using a blind. This first player, being the blind, is required to make a $5 blind bet. He promptly does so, flipping a $5 chip into the pot. All bets before the draw in draw poker, high or low, are in the lower tier of the betting limit. In this example, all bets and raises are in $5 increments.

The next player to act sits at the blind's left, since play in all poker variations proceeds in a clockwise direction. He has three choices. He can call the $5 blind bet and remain an active player, raise that bet $5 more and place $10 into the pot, or fold his cards. Play proceeds around the table until all players have made their decisions—either to call the blind and any raises made, or to fold and wait for the next cycle of poker life to begin.

The draw occurs in the same order as the betting and dealing of the cards. The blind, if he is still in the pot, goes first. He can exchange up to five cards for new ones. Each active player, in turn, can exchange as many of his original cards as he likes, but he should do so only after the preceding player has received his cards. Discards should be announced so that all players are aware of the number of cards each person has drawn. Players who elect to stand pat (not draw any cards) can indicate this verbally or by knocking on the table with their fists.

After the draw is completed, the second and last betting round occurs. It is begun by the blind, or, if he has folded, by the first active player closest to the dealer's left. All bets and raises in this round are in the upper tier of the $5-$10 limit, in $10 increments. If the game were a $3-$6 game, all bets after the draw would be in $6 increments.

After the betting round is completed, there is the showdown, where the lowest hand collects the pot and all the money in it. If, at any point in the game, all opponents drop out of play, the remaining player would be the automatic winner, and he claims the pot. The deal now moves to the left. In the case of a casino game, the former blind is now the button, and can enjoy all the advantages of playing the dealer's position.

STRATEGY FOR LOWBALL
Lowball gives the knowledgeable player a tremendous advantage over uninitiated opponents, since the strategic thinking is different in this poker variation. Players are shooting for different types of hands, and it takes the high poker player a while to become accustomed to the peculiarities of the game.

The first rule in lowball is never to play a hand which needs more than one card drawn to improve to a winner. Unlike high poker, draws of two or even three cards are terrible draws and immediately single out a player as a weak opponent. A two-card draw is a shot in the dark. It's equivalent to trying to fill a three-card straight in high poker.

To win at lowball, you must start out with cards that can win. If the cards you're dealt are weak, throw them away unless you can get a free ride. For example, if you're the blind, and there are no raises following the forced bet, it costs nothing more to play, so you should stay in for the draw. Always play further if there is no cost, no matter the cards. If you're faced with a bet, however, fold, unless you've got the goods.

Position is important in lowball and must be considered in the opening strategies. Here are my minimum opening cards in lowball:

Lowball · Minimum Starting Cards

First Four Positions: (Early)	8-high—pat hand 7-high—one card draw
Second Two Positions: (Middle)	9-high—pat hand 8-high—one card draw
Last Two Positions: (Late)	10-high—pat hand 9-high—one card draw

Unless you hold an 8-high pat hand or have a four-card 7-high in early position, you can't call the blind's bet or make an opener yourself. You must fold. You're too vulnerable to raises behind your position to call with these hands in the first four spots. There is a strong possibility that players will up the stakes in the middle and late positions. It is foolish to call hands in middle and early position if you will be forced to fold on a raise. Do not call bets with anything less than the minimum openers in early and middle positions. In late position, if a bet and a raise have preceded your play, call with a minimum holding of an 8-high pat hand or a four card 7-high draw.

With a 7-high pat hand, you hold a strong hand and should play aggressively. Raise the opener from any position at the table. If a raiser precedes you, re-raise. When you're dealt a 6-high pat hand, you have almost a sure winner. Don't raise in early position. You want to keep as many players as possible in the game. If, however, a player raises behind you, and it's just you and he and maybe one other player, re-raise and build up the pot. There's something pleasurable about winning big pots.

5. SEVEN-CARD STUD

Seven-card stud's three main variations—high, low (also called Razz), and high-low—all pack into play five exciting betting rounds. In each variation, players form their best five-card combination out of the seven dealt to produce their final hands.

In **seven- card high stud**, the highest ranking hand remaining wins the pot. In **seven-card low stud**, the lowest hand claims the gold. In **high-low stud**, players vie for either the highest-ranking or lowest-ranking hand, with the best of each claiming half the pot, or players can go for the high-low pot and risk all to win all. Once again, players also can win the pot by being the last remaining player in the pot— either as a result of skillful bluffing or by attrition of opponents due to stiff betting.

In each variation, players receive seven cards. After the first three cards are dealt, two face-down (closed) and one face-up (open), the first betting round commences. The following three cards are dealt open, one-at-a-time, with a betting round accompanying each card. The last card, the seventh, comes "down and dirty." It's the third closed card received by the players.

All remaining players now hold three hole cards and four open cards. These are the final cards they will hold. One more round of betting follows the seventh card. Then the showdown occurs, and the best hand or hands (as may be the case in high-low) claims the pot.

THE PLAY OF THE GAME

Following the shuffle and the cut, the cards are dealt in a clockwise direction beginning with the player to the dealer's left and continuing around the table, in order, until all players have received two closed cards and one open card. The two face down cards are called **hole cards**, as is the seventh card, also closed, that the player receives last.

All antes, if required, should be placed into the pot before the cards are dealt. Once an ante reaches the pot, it is like any other bet. It is the property of the pot and will belong to the eventual winner of the hand.

PRIVATE HIGH AND HIGH-LOW GAMES

In the private high and high-low seven-card stud games, the player with the highest ranking open card starts the betting. If two or more players hold equivalent values, the high-card player closest to the dealer's left must bet to open play on **third street**, the name for this betting round, the first in seven-card stud. It is a required wager. There is no checking on this round. Subsequent players must either call the bet, raise, or fold.

On all following rounds, the highest ranking open hand opens the play. From **fourth street** (the name for the second betting round in seven card stud) on, the high hand may check to open betting. It is only on the first betting round that the opening bet is mandatory.

CASINO HIGH GAMES

In casino versions of seven-card high stud, unlike in private games, the player holding the lowest open card must open betting. When two players have identically valued low cards, the player with the lower ranked suit plays first. For this purpose only, the suits are ranked in order of strength, beginning with spades, the highest, and followed in descending order by hearts, diamonds, and clubs.

For example, if the lowest cards showing are the 3♣ and the 3♥, the 3♣ will open the betting. As in the private game, in the first round of play, the player who goes first is required to make an opening bet, and all following players, in turn, must call, raise, or fold. In subsequent rounds, the player holding the highest ranking open hand acts first, and he may check or bet to begin play.

CASINO HIGH-LOW GAMES

In casino high-low seven-card stud, the lowest card

opens the betting in the first round of play, and it's a mandatory bet. Thereafter, in all future rounds, the high hand acts first, and may begin play by checking or betting as desired.

PRIVATE AND CASINO LOW GAMES

In private seven-card low stud games, the player holding the lowest open card (the ace counts as the lowest card in low poker) acts first and must make the mandatory opening bet. Conversely, in the casino games of seven-card low stud, the highest ranking open card makes the required opening bet. There is no first round checking in these games either—players must call the opener, raise, or fold.

In all subsequent rounds, in the private and casino versions of seven-card low stud, the lowest ranking open hand acts first and may check or bet as desired. For example, a player showing 8 6 2 A on board, an 8 6 hand, opens against a player showing a pair of 6s, 6 6 3 2, while a 6 4 2 A board would open against a 7 3 2 A.

EXAMPLE GAME

Let's look at how the betting works in seven-card poker using a $5-$10 high stud game as an example. In the private game, the high-card player must make a set bet, in this case $5. If the game were $1-$2, the opener would be $1, and in a $15-$30 game, $15 would be the opener. Subsequent players must either call that $5 bet, fold, or, if they want, raise that bet by $5 to make it $10 to the next player. All bets and raises in this first betting round, called third street, are in $5 increments, the lower limit of the $5-$10 betting tier.

The casino $5-$10 game varies slightly. There, the forced opening bet, called the **blind**, is a $1 bet, and the first raise is $3 only. (These numbers may vary depending upon the casino, but they are always lower than the lower limit.) Thereafter, all bets and raises this round are in $5 increments. For example, if the opening $1 bet was raised $3 by the second player to act, the third player needs to call the $1 blind and the $3 raise, a total of $4 to stay in the pot. If the third player raises as well, his raise would have to be $5. The next player would need to call $9 worth of bets and raises to play.

When play returns to the opener in either the casino or private game, the opener must call all raises that succeeded his opener to stay in the game, as would any player who also had a raise follow his or her position. In the above example, the opener needs to call the $3 and $5 raises to play, while the second player, the first raiser, must call just the $5 raise.

The next betting round is called fourth street. Each active player receives a face-up card. Everyone now holds a total of four cards, two open and two closed. Play in this round, as in all future rounds, is the same in both the casino and private versions. It begins with the player holding the highest ranking hand on board (or, in low poker, the lowest ranking), and moves clockwise around the table. When two or more players hold identically ranked cards, the player closest to the dealer's left will play first.

All bets and raises this round are in $5 increments unless an open pair shows on board, in which case players can open with a $10 bet. From fourth street on, the opening player is not forced to make a bet. He may open betting by just checking. It is only on third street that an opening bet is required.

Once fourth street betting is concluded, another open card is dealt. Players now have a total of three face up cards in addition to their two down cards. This round is called **fifth street**, and all bets and raises on this round and on the following two rounds—sixth and seventh streets—are in $10 increments, the upper tier of the $5-$10 betting limit. (In a $3-$6 game, bets would be in $6 increments, and in a $15-$30 games, $30 increments.)

After fifth street betting closes, players receive their fourth open card. This next betting round is called **sixth street**, since all remaining players now have a total of six cards.

Seventh street is the next round, and each remaining player receives his last card face down. This is the final betting round in seven-card stud, and it's followed by the showdown. Each player chooses five cards out of the seven total he holds to form his best hand. In seven-card high stud, the best high hand wins, and in the lower stud version, the five best low cards will claim the pot.

Let's examine the showdown in seven-card high-low stud to see how it differs from the high and low stud variations.

THE SHOWDOWN: SEVEN-CARD HIGH-LOW STUD

Seven-card high-low stud is played similarly to the high or low seven card stud games. The major difference is that players are actually playing for two halves of the pot: half the pot goes to the player with the best high hand and the other half goes to the player holding the strongest low hand. If a player holds the best high and the best low hand, he will take the entire pot.

High-low seven-card stud is played as either declaration or cards speak. In **declaration**, which is predominantly played in private poker games, players declare at the showdown whether they're going for the high, the low, or the high-low end of the pot.

Declaration is accomplished by each player hiding a colored chip in his fist and extending his closed fist over the table. At a given signal, players simultaneously open their hands and reveal their declarations. White chips are usually used for a low declaration, blue chips for high, and red chips for high-low, though using coins or different color assignments will work just as well for the declaration.

Among the players who declared "high," the best high hand wins that half of the pot, while the best low hand among players who declared "low" takes the other half. If just one player calls "high" and the rest "low," the player declaring high automatically wins half the pot and need not show his hand, while the low callers must compete for their half with the best low total winning. And vice versa. If all players declare the same way, for example, all declare high, then the best high hand wins the entire pot. If all players declared low, then the best low hand claims the entire pot.

Players that declare "high-low" risk all, and must win both the best high hand *and* the best low hand or they forfeit the entire pot. It's an all or nothing proposition—they either win it all or lose it all. If a high-low declarer wins only one way, then he's out of the pot, and the best high hand and the best low hand split the monies.

Let's follow an illustrative showdown in a game being played as declaration. Five players remain: Donto, Fay, Julian, Eddie-boy, and Big Phil. The first three declare "high," the fourth "low," and the fifth, Big Phil, goes all out and declares "high-low." (Flavian has already folded and both he and his cigar watch passively from the sidelines.)

Here are the hands they hold:

Donto (Declared high)	J♣ 10♠ 9♦ 8♥ 7♣
Fay (Declared high)	K♥ K♣ K♦ 5♣ 4♥
Julian (Declared high)	A♦ 10♦ 8♦ 6♦ 3♦
Eddie-boy (Declared low)	7♦ 6♥ 4♣ 3♥ 2♥
Big Phil (Declared high-low)	High: K♠ 7♠ 5♠ 4♠ 2♠
	Low: 7♠ 5♠ 4♠ 3♣ 2♠

Big Phil's 7 5 hand is a stronger low than Eddie-boy's 7 6, but his king-high flush is weaker than Julian's ace-high flush. Therefore, Big Phil, unable to win both ways, loses his high-low declaration and wins nothing. Julian and Eddie-boy hold the best high and low hands respectively, and they split the pot. Had Big Phil declared "low" only, he would have won that half of the pot.

In **cards speak**, also called **high-low split**, the seven card high-low stud game played in the Nevada casinos, there is no declaration at the showdown. Players simply reveal their cards. The best high hand and the best low hand split the pot, or, if one player is fortunate enough to have the best high and low, he claims it all.

STRATEGY FOR SEVEN-CARD STUD: HIGH POKER

The first three cards you receive in seven-card stud lay the groundwork for the future possibilities of your hand. Therefore, to build winners, you should stay in only with cards that have the right winning ingredients. Starting and staying with promising cards is especially important in seven-card stud, since the five betting rounds of this game add up to a lot of bets and raises. You want to give yourself every chance of winning.

These are the minimum starting cards you need to enter the betting in seven-card high stud:

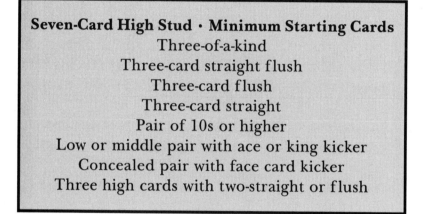

Seven-Card High Stud · Minimum Starting Cards
Three-of-a-kind
Three-card straight flush
Three-card flush
Three-card straight
Pair of 10s or higher
Low or middle pair with ace or king kicker
Concealed pair with face card kicker
Three high cards with two-straight or flush

Starting cards of three-of-a-kind are powerful cards and are heavily favored to win. With these cards, you want to keep as many players in the pot as possible. Play low key on third and fourth street, calling bets but not raising. Later, on fifth street, if your opponents start showing threatening signs of flushes or straights, bet heavy. You should either force them out or make them pay for the privilege of trying to buy their hands. If your trips turn into a full house, however, you have nothing to fear from straights or flushes. You want them filling their straights and flushes—and how!

With three-card flushes and straights, call third street betting, but do not raise. In general, with poker strategies, it is prudent to raise only when you've either got the goods or are bluffing (and only under the right circumstances!) If your three-card straight or flush doesn't improve by fourth street, it's time to say goodbye. Fold the hand. The odds against filling it are getting too steep for the cost of calling bets and chasing cards for three more betting rounds. You must also fold medium pairs that haven't improved by fourth street if either a higher pair shows on board or raises precede your turn.

A key element in winning at seven-card stud, or at any poker game for that matter, is to lose as little as possible in the deals you don't win. You must fold hands which have not panned out or have become underdogs. Avoid the temptation to play "just one more card." That one more card costs money, and if it's not a sound call, it's a bet deducted from your overall winnings.

To be a winner, you must wager with the odds, not against them. And those odds are defined by the cards held vis-a-vis our opponents, not based on the hopes of what might happen "if." Again, when a hand's possibilities fade and it becomes second best, bury it.

One indicator of how powerful hands may be going into the showdown is the intensity of the betting. If betting is heavy, with raises and re-raises, there is probably a reason. Expect to see strong cards at the show down. If betting is light, with just a few players left, the average winning hand will probably be less powerful than otherwise.

It is important to play alertly and be aware of all cards that are dealt open in seven-card stud. These cards provide lots of information on the possibilities of improving your hand or on the chances of an opponent improving his hand or having certain cards in the hole. For example, if an opponent holds an open pair of kings and earlier you saw two kings folded, you know that no matter what kind of luck that player has, there's no way he can buy a third king. On the other hand, you'll be more hesitant playing for a flush if you realize that six of the clubs you need have already been played. Heads up play is important in seven-card stud and will make a big difference toward more profitable winning sessions.

STRATEGY FOR SEVEN-CARD STUD: LOW POKER (RAZZ)

In seven-card low stud, players use their best five cards out of the seven dealt to form the lowest hand possible, as opposed to high stud, where players look to form their highest totals. (See the section on lowball in the draw poker chapter for ranking hands in low poker.) Strategic thinking in razz is different than in high poker. Good lowball hands always start out as **drawing hands**, hands which need advantageous draws to develop into winners.

Your first four cards may be A 2 3 4, a golden start, but if the following three cards you receive are a pair of jacks and a king, then your hand melts into nothing. On the other hand, seven-card high stud presents situations where you're dealt lock hands for starters, such as the starting hand K K K. Regardless of future draws, these trip kings are heavily favored to win. Subsequent draws cannot diminish the inherent strength of those cards. In contrast, lowball hands which don't pan out die on the vine and become worthless.

To be competitive in seven-card lowball, you must, nonetheless, enter the betting with strong starting cards, ones that can go all the way. Following are the minimum opening or calling hands that should be played in Razz.

Seven-Card Low Stud · Minimum Starting Cards

Three-card 7-high or better (lower)
Three-card 8-high with two cards valued 5 or lower
Three-card 9-high with the other card as ace, 2, or 3
An ace plus a 5 or a lower card, and an odd card.

If you don't hold one of the above combinations, you must fold. You don't want to play underdog cards and contribute to other players' pots. If you can get a free ride into fourth street, take it, but hands of less than the above-mentioned caliber cannot call a blind or opening bet. However, if you're the blind, and no raises occur behind your position, you're already in—take the free card on fourth street.

Relatively low supporting cards in low poker are called **smooth** hands, such as the trey (3) and deuce (2) in the starting hand of 7 3 2, or the 4, 3, 2, and ace in the hand 8 4 3 2 A, a *smooth eight*. Hands where the supporting cards are relatively high are called **rough**, such as the 6 and 4 in the starting cards 7 6 4, called a *rough seven*, or the 7, 5, 4, and 3 in the hand 8 7 5 4 3, a *rough eight*. Smooth hands have greater possibilities than their rough counterparts. You should play them more aggressively.

If you make an 8-high hand or a smooth 9 on fifth street, you're in a strong position. You can play forcefully against players still holding drawing hands. You should raise their drawing hands. You're the favorite, and you either want to force them out of the pot or make them pay for every card they try to buy. Play aggressively against weak players. They'll stay in too long with inferior hands. When you've got the goods, why not make your winning pot that much larger?

STRATEGY FOR SEVEN-CARD STUD: HIGH-LOW POKER

The splitting of the pot into two halves, one for the best high hand and one for the best low, makes seven-card stud an action-packed and exciting game.

An astute player can win healthy sums against loose opponents.

Though there are more ways to win at high-low stud, you must not let the increased opportunities of winning pots tempt you into looser playing habits. The same winning principles apply—enter the betting only with good starting cards, ones which hold possibilities of winning either the high or low end of the pot.

Straddling the middle with hands that hold both high and low possibilities but are mediocre in both directions is a costly and weak strategy. You can work only with the cards that you're dealt. If the hand is not strong as either a high or low hand, then the cards should be folded. Save your bets and play only with cards that can make you a winner.

Enter the betting with the same starting cards you would play in either high seven-card stud for the high pot or in Razz for the low pot. If your cards develop into potential two-way winners, that's even better. For now, though, concentrate on winning at least one way.

SEVEN-CARD STUD

Here are the minimum starting cards needed to play for the low pot:

Seven-Card High-Low Stud ·
Minimum Low-End Starting Cards

Three card 7-high or lower
Three card 8-high containing two cards 5 or less
Three card 9-high, with the two back-up cards being an ace, 2 or 3

With three promising low cards, play till fourth street, but if you don't receive a fourth low card, fold. You have to face three more betting rounds, and with heavy betting and raising, trying to catch two more low cards is an expensive proposition, especially with only half a pot as the prize. However, if other low hand possibilities haven't improved either, and it seems your hand is still a competitor for the low pot, fifth street could be worth a play.

Low hands with flush or straight possibilities, such as the 7 5 2 of hearts or 5 4 3 of mixed suits, are ideal high-low hands. They provide the double threat of taking the high and low pots, and, if the cards pan out, of winning the high-low pot outright.

Here are the minimum starting hands for the high pot:

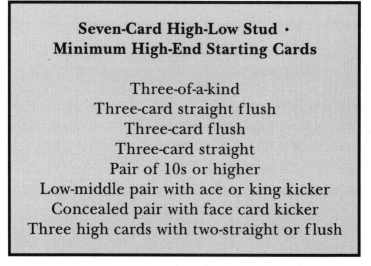

**Seven-Card High-Low Stud ·
Minimum High-End Starting Cards**

Three-of-a-kind
Three-card straight flush
Three-card flush
Three-card straight
Pair of 10s or higher
Low-middle pair with ace or king kicker
Concealed pair with face card kicker
Three high cards with two-straight or flush

You can also play a concealed low pair, 7s or lower, with a low open card, 6 or lower, until fourth street. If the hand doesn't improve there, that hand should be folded. Though you'll go in with a lot of hands, you'll also be quick to fold many of them if there is no improvement on fourth street.

Three-card flushes and straights should be ditched if the fourth card isn't bought, unless fourth street position leaves you with a combination three-flush or straight and three-card 7-high low hand. In that case, take the hand to fifth street, and stay there only if you improve to a four-card low or four-card flush or straight. Otherwise, fold the hand.

Low or medium pairs that don't improve should

be thrown away. With only half a pot to win, the odds don't justify playing these marginal cards. Similarly, the three high-card hand, two-straight, and two-flush hands should be thrown away if they don't improve.

The nature of high-low stud calls for more aggressive play. When you have a lock on either the high or low end of the pot, bet forcefully. You want to create big pots and make the winnings that much sweeter.

6. HOLD 'EM

Hold 'em, or **Texas hold 'em**, as the game is sometimes called, is steadily growing in popularity, and is perhaps best associated with freewheeling high action poker. Players receive two face-down cards. They combine these with the five face-up community cards shared by all the players to form their best five-card hand. Altogether, hold 'em has four betting rounds. At the showdown, the highest ranking hand wins the pot. If heavy betting has forced out all opponents, the last remaining player wins.

THE PLAY OF THE GAME

The dealer deals cards one at a time, beginning with the player at the button or dealer's left, and proceeding clockwise, until all players have received two face down cards. The player to the left of the dealer goes first in this round. He is known as the **small blind**. The player to his left goes next, and he is known as the **big blind**.

Both these players must make "blind" bets—mandatory opening wagers that create immediate action since succeeding players are forced to call them to remain active. The small blind is normally smaller

HOLD 'EM

than the lower range bet in limit poker, while the big blind is typically equal to the lower range bet. For example, in a $3-$6 limit game, the small blind might be a $1 bet, and the big blind would be $3.

The required blinds can vary. Some hold 'em games may even play with no blind; in these instances players must either bet or fold. Blind or no blind, checking is not allowed on the first round of hold 'em.

In casino games, a button is used to simulate the dealer's position, since a house employee actually deals the game. The button is moved clockwise around the table after each deal so that every player in turn gets to be the imaginary dealer and can benefit from that advantageous position.

Let's look at a $3-$6 limit game to see how the betting goes. The first player to act sits to the dealer's left. He must open betting by placing a $1 blind into the pot. This is a forced wager, and he must make it regardless of how poor his cards might be. The player at the blind's left must either call this $1 blind, raise it $2, or fold. If this player folds, each succeeding player is faced with the same options: call, raise, or fold.

If the blind gets raised $2, the next player must either call the $3 ($1 blind plus $2 raise), raise $3 to make the total bet $6 to the following player, or fold. After the $1 blind and initial $2 raise, all further raises during this round must be in $3 increments. The maximum number of raises permitted during a round is generally between three and five raises. If no player has called the $1 blind bet, the blind wins the antes. The deal passes on clockwise to the next player for the next hand.

Once the initial betting round is over, three cards are turned face up in the center of the table. Known as the **flop**, these cards are used by all the players. Each player now has five cards to form a hand—his two hole cards and three community cards.

The next round of betting begins. This is called third street, and it also starts with the blind. If he has dropped, the player in the next active position to his left begins this betting round. Bets and raises during this round are in $3 increments only. In a $5-$10 game, bets and raises would be limited to $5 increments, and in a $15-$30 game, $15 increments.

On the following round, **fourth street**, a fourth community card is dealt face up on the table. It's called the **turn**. Players now have a total of six cards possible to form their best five. Betting in this round and on the following round, fifth street, begins with the blind. If he has folded, the next active player to his left begins the betting, which is in the upper limit. In the $3-$6 game, all bets and raises are in $6 increments, while in the $5-$10 game, bets and raises would be in $10 increments, and in a $15-$30 game, $30 increments.

There is no forced opening bet on fourth street (or fifth street, which follows), and the first player to act may check to open play. Subsequent players may check as well. If all players check, then the betting round is over and fifth street play will follow. However, should a player open betting on fourth street, all active players must call that bet to remain in the pot. On fourth street and fifth street, all bets are in the upper tier of the betting range. In a $3-$6 game, the opening bet and all future raises must be in $6 increments.

After fourth street betting, the fifth and final community card, called the river, will be turned over in the center of the table. Players now combine their two hole cards with five of the community cards to form their best and final five-card hand. At **fifth street**, which is what this round is called, there is one final betting round, followed by the showdown. The highest ranking hand wins at the showdown. If all opponents have folded, the last remaining player wins the pot by default, and collects all the antes, bets, and raises that were made.

STRATEGY FOR HOLD 'EM

The first two cards in hold 'em, the player's down cards, along with his position at the table, are the most important considerations in strategy. As in all poker variations, players must start with solid cards to give themselves the best chances of winning. We'll divide the starting hands into four different categories: strongest, strong, marginal, and weak.

HOW TO PLAY WINNING POKER

STRONGEST STARTING HANDS IN HOLD 'EM

These hands are listed in descending order, best hand first:

AA
KK
AK (suited)
QQ
AQ (suited)
AK

The above six starting card combinations are the best in hold 'em. They are strong enough to call from any position at the table, and you should play them aggressively. Excellent starting cards in hold 'em, more than in any other poker variation, will hold up and finish as winners, so with these cards you'll be raising at the first opportunity.

You're the favorite in this game, and you want to build up the pot. At the same time, though, you want to force out players with strong or marginal hands. If the cost to play is too cheap, more players will take a shot at the flop. The more players who stay in the pot, the greater the risk is that a weaker hand will draw out and beat your favorite.

STRONG STARTING HANDS IN HOLD 'EM

These hands are also listed in descending order:

AQ
AJ (suited)
A10 (suited)
KQ (suited)

Hands of an ace plus a high card are powerful combinations in hold 'em. If the flop, fourth, or fifth street shows an ace, these paired aces tower over any kings, queens, or lesser pairs that other players may hold. It's tough to play picture pairs against an ace flop; you've got to figure at least one opponent for a hidden ace. Since only the best hand wins, you must fold lesser pairs against an open ace.

Suited high cards are strong because they give a player the twin chance of forming a high pair or suiting up to a possible flush. You can play the hands in the strong category from any position. Though they're not as strong as the hands in the "strongest" group, you should still play them aggressively for maximum value.

MARGINAL STARTING HANDS IN HOLD 'EM

These hands are listed in descending order, best hand first:

JJ
AJ
KQ
A10
KJ (suited)
1010
QJ (suited)
K10 (suited)
KJ
Q10 (suited)
99

Play your marginal hands in hold 'em as you would play marginal hands in the other poker variations—stay in only if the cost is cheap. These hands have possibilities, but they're not worth the price of a stiff bet. To enter the betting with marginal hands, you must take into account your position at the table.

The last position is the best. It permits you to see what prior bets were made before committing your hand. When you're facing heavy bets and raises, you must fold marginal hands. If only a call is necessary, however, give these cards a chance at the flop. A good flop can turn these cards into favorites.

In early or middle position, if you're holding marginal hands, you can call the opening bet. If there's been a raise, though, you must fold. If there is a raise after the initial bet has been called, you can see this raise also, but you must fold in the face of a double raise, or in situations where yet another raise can follow.

WEAK HANDS

All other hands, ones not shown in the above three categories, should be folded. They are heavy underdogs with little chances of winning. If you're playing in a hold 'em game requiring a blind or opening bet, by all means, though, take the flop for free. If it costs you to see the flop, fold immediately. It's much cheaper watching this round as a bystander.

7. OMAHA

A relatively new form of poker that took hold in cardrooms and casinos in the 1990's is the very exciting game of Omaha. Action is plentiful, especially in the high-low variations, where multi-way pots and frequent raising make the game very exciting. More and more players are finding that Omaha is their game of choice.

Players will choose from a total pool of nine cards to form their best five-card hands. Four of these cards will be in their own possession, dealt to them as down cards, while five cards will be face up in the community pool to be shared by all. Players may not choose just any of the nine cards for their final five-card hands. They must use two cards from their own set of four cards and three from the community pool. Thus, if a player were dealt four aces in the hole, only two of the aces would count toward the final hand. The remaining three cards would have to come from the board.

In the case of Omaha high-low, players can choose two different sets of cards to make their final hands, one set for the high hand and one set for the low hand. For example, if a player held Q Q 5 2, and the board showed Q K A 7 6, two queens from his cards would be used to form the hand Q Q Q A K— three queens with ace and king kickers for high. His 5 and 2 would be used to form 7 6 5 2 Q for low. In both of these instances, as you see, two of the player's down cards and three community cards were used to make the final poker hand.

THE PLAY OF THE GAME

In casino games, a button is used to simulate the dealers position, since a house employee actually deals the game. It is moved clockwise around the table after each deal, so that every player in turn gets to play the dealer's position and can benefit from that advantage. As in hold 'em, position is extremely important in the Omaha games. The player on the button is in the best spot.

Each player starts by receiving four cards dealt face-down, one at a time, from the dealer. Again, the deal begins with the player at the button or dealer's left. It proceeds clockwise, until all players have received their allotment. There are normally two blinds in the casino games, a small blind and a big blind. The **small blind**—the player to the left of the button position—goes first, and the **big blind**—the player to his left—goes next.

As in all poker games, all action proceeds clockwise around the table. The order of receiving cards and betting remains the same throughout the deal. The button will always act last, and the first active player to the button's left will always go first. Unlike seven-card stud, where the order of betting changes depending upon what cards are held on board, in Omaha, position remains constant throughout a deal. When a hand is completed, the button will move one place to the left, and for that deal the order of betting again would remain constant in the deal.

The big blind, the second bet, is normally equal to the lower range bet in limit Omaha, while the small blind is less than that amount. For example, in a $15-$30 limit game, the big blind would be $15. The amount of the blinds can vary from game to game. Again, after the blinds are made, each succeeding player must either call these blinds to stay active, raise the blinds, or fold. All bets in this round must be in the lower increment of the two-tier structure: $15 in a $15-$30 game, $5 in $5-$10, $50 in $50-$100, and so on.

Once all betting has been completed, three cards are turned face up in the center of the table. This is the **flop**, to be shared by all players. There is another round of betting, starting with the small blind. If he has dropped, betting begins with the big blind, or the player in the next active position to his left. (The blinds may have folded due to raises after their plays.)

The first player to act may bet or check as he pleases—there is no forced blind bet in this round, or the future betting rounds. It is only in the first betting round, when the initial four cards are dealt, that there is a blind. In fact, all players can check across the board if they so please. Of course, though, once a bet is made, succeeding players must call that bet (and raises if made), or they must fold their cards. As in the first round of betting, all bets are again at the lower increment. In a $10-$20 game, bets and raises would be for $10. If the game were $3-$6, they would be for $3.

When betting is completed, a fourth community card is dealt face-up. This is **fourth street**. There's another round of betting. Then comes **fifth street**, where the fifth and final community card is dealt face-up in the middle of the table for all to share. Betting on fourth and fifth streets is in the upper limit of the two-tier structure. In the $5-$10 game, bets and raises would be in $10 increments, and in a $15-$30 game, $30 increments.

Fifth street marks the last card the players will receive and the last betting round. Now comes the showdown. Players combine their best two hole cards with three of the five community cards to form their best and final five-card hand. The highest ranking hand wins at the showdown. If all opponents have folded, the last remaining player wins the pot by default. He collects all the antes, bets, and raises that were made.

OMAHA

OMAHA HIGH

In the high version, the highest ranking hand wins all the money at the showdown. If this player's best five cards are equal to an opponent's, they will split the pot equally.

OMAHA HIGH-LOW 8 OR BETTER

In Omaha High-Low 8 or Better, there are often split pots at the showdown. In fact, there are often multiple split pots. For example, if two low hands are tied for best, and there is a high-hand winner, the high hand will take half the pot, and the two low players will get *quartered*—each of them will split the low half, or get one quarter of the total pot.

If there happened to be three low winners, they would split the low end three ways, or get one-sixth of the pot each, with the high side winner taking sole possession of the high half of the pot. Ties for high would be split the same way—all winners get an equal portion from the high half of the pot, or from the whole pot if no player qualifies for low.

For there to be a winner on the low end, that hand must be no worse than 8 or better. For example, a player would need to hold, say, 8 7 5 3 A to qualify. A hand of 9 7 3 2 A would not qualify, even though it may be the lowest hand. Instead, the high end winner or winners would get all the spoils.

As I've said, to qualify for the best five-card hand, a player must use two cards from his four cards and three from the community cards. Thus, a player holding 2 3 4 6 with a community board of A 7 10 J K would not have a qualified low hand since only the 2 and 3 could be used from his own cards.

In casino games, **cards speak** determines the best hands at the showdown, while in private games, there is often a **declare**, with players announcing which part of the pot they're going for. Thus, if a player declares low in a private game and doesn't have the best low, that player wins nothing, even if he happened to have the best high hand. If he declared both ways, high-low, and won only one of the ways, he would also lose the entire pot. In the casino game, the cards themselves will determine the winners and losers.

STRATEGY FOR OMAHA HIGH-LOW 8 OR BETTER

Omaha High-Low 8 or Better is a free-wheeling game, and chips come in from all directions. With both a high pot and low pot to go after, many players stay interested in the pot, especially since the river card on fifth street can so dramatically change a player's possibilities of winning.

The first four cards dealt in Omaha—your down cards—are the only cards you alone use, and thus are very important in determining your chances of winning. As in all poker variations, you must start out with solid cards to give yourself the best chances of winning.

OMAHA

There are great starting cards, good starting cards, and poor starting cards, as in other poker games, but what appears to be good or bad pre-flop may change in a flash when the flop throws three more cards into the mix. Then there are two more community cards that will fall, opening up even more possibilities and making and breaking other hands.

With such a wide range of possibilities, hopes stay high for players, and betting can be fierce. Thus, one of the key strategies to follow in this version of Omaha is to play on the tight side. Don't get sucked into the rampant betting that sometimes occurs, not unless your possibilities are good enough. Speculation can lose you a bunch of money in a hurry in this game.

Another major consideration in Omaha High-Low 8 or Better is your position at the table. Since it stays constant throughout a round, and leverage is everything in Omaha, all plays must be made with position being foremost on your mind.

Starting hands with two very low cards give you a strong starting position in Omaha. An ace and a 2 are good, since if three low cards fall on the flop, you have the nut low with two more betting rounds to go. Or if two low cards fall on the flop (say it is 3 7 J), you just need one more non-pairing low card for the nut low. Other starters such as 2 3, 3 4, A 3, or A 4 are also good cards to have. They put you in good position to go for low.

Since low hands can be quartered, the best starters in Omaha 8 high-low would be ones that gave you both high and low possibilities. Consecutive suited low cards, such as A 2, 2 3, 3 4, give you excellent chances of going low and wheeling or flushing to a high hand. Combine these low cards with A A or A K, and these two way hands hold out many possibilities. The hand A K 2 3 with suited cards is very powerful, with nut high and nut low straight possibilities. A 2 3 4 suited gives nut low and wheel possibilities. High starting hands of A A K Q and A A K K can hold strong if the flop is all high cards, preventing low hands from taking half the pot.

The relative value of high hands relates to the flop not only for the cards and possibilities it gives both you and your opponents, but also for the chances it gives players to form low hands, which immediately devalue the pot by one half. This is a key concept that players going for the high end of the pot must consider in Omaha. For example, for any player to qualify for a low total, there would have to be three low cards on board. If three low cards (8 or below) appear, it is likely that one player has a valid low. But if two low cards or fewer are on board, there will be no low hand, and the high hand will take the whole pot.

Thus, when making your decision on how to play a high hand, you must consider its strength on a different relative merit than straight high games if there will be a low hand grabbing half that pot. The pot is now worth *half* of what you might normally expect. This greatly affects the pot odds and how you need to view your high position.

When low cards will cut into your pot and take half of your action, you need a higher winning expectation and assurance of taking the high half to make the betting profitable. The great danger in high-low games that regular high or low players don't consider is this dilution of the pot, which makes betting and playing strategy considerations fundamentally different. That is why hands with the strength to go both ways are so valuable in high-low games.

8. THE 15 WINNING CONCEPTS OF POKER

The knowledgeable player can consistently make money playing poker, but only if he approaches the game from the proper perspective. As in any game of skill, there are important concepts that you must follow to be a winner. In this chapter, we'll discuss these concepts. I'll show you how to recognize and implement the general winning concepts of poker to get an edge on your opponents and be a winner.

I've divided this chapter into fifteen winning concepts to isolate the factors that will improve your play and increase your winnings at the table. You'll learn how to analyze situations and determine whether the relative strength of your hand is strong enough to call a bet or even raise. Sometimes, because of the bet size, the amount of money in the pot, your position at the table, or your knowledge of your opponents' playing styles, you're better off folding the hand and conceding the pot.

A poker session is an accumulation of hands won and lost. To come out an overall winner, you must maximize your gains when you win and minimize losses when you lose so that the winnings overshadow the losses and you have a profit to show. Of course, you never really know until the showdown whether you're holding the winning hand, but you can approximate your relative standing in the game and adjust your play accordingly. Thus, when you're the favorite to win you'll get as much mileage out of the hand as you can. Let's now get down to the winning concepts of play.

WINNING CONCEPT #1: Play Against Competition You Can Beat

As with everything, being "good" at poker is relative. You may be a winning player at $5-$10, but if you moved your chips to a $50-$100 game, you might get eaten alive. Similarly, while you may be a good basketball player at your local park, or a good chess player in your local club, if you started playing against the pros, you'd be lucky to be thought a scrub. Even the pros you might encounter wouldn't be good enough to be on the court with Michael Jordan or across the board from Garry Kasparov.

The point is, you can't win at poker unless you're playing against competition at or below your level. If you play over your head, well, you'll be over your head. The game will be a one-sided affair, and you'll be on the losing end. So, rule number one, play with players you *can* beat. Don't be a patsy for players who are just too good for you. Don't play at a higher stakes game unless you're able to beat the level of game you currently play.

The converse of that statement holds true as well: if you're unable to beat the level of game at which you currently play, don't move up a level thinking your "luck" will change. The only thing that will happen is that even better players will take your money at a faster clip. You'll be over your head. Move down instead. Get to a level where you can swim. You want to be the shark making money, not the fish being eaten.

For example, if you're at a $15-$30 game, and you're constantly taking a beating, you're not ready for the game yet. Why take the punishment? Get to the $5-$10 game, where your skills may be more equal to the competition. Improve your game there.

Take each level of poker game in stride. You can make more money at a higher stakes game, but only if you're good enough to beat that game. A busy cardroom may offer games for $1-3, $5-$10, $15-$30, $30-$60, $50-$100, $150-$300, or even higher. Just because higher stakes games are there doesn't mean you have to play them. Go slow, and work your way up as your skills improve.

WINNING CONCEPT #2: Fold When You're Beat!

Winning money in poker is not just about winning pots. In fact, being an overall winning player probably has more to do with losing less when your cards don't come in the running than it has to do with the pots you win when you have the best hand! Many players don't appreciate this concept. Despite winning enough pots, they can't understand why they keep leaving the table with losses.

Folding when you're beaten at the table is one of the most important concepts in poker. More money is lost by players who consistently make bet after bet in clearly losing situations than in possibly any other aspect of poker. Every extra bet you contribute to an opponent's pot is a bet out of your stack.

> *It's as important to make good folds in poker as it is to make good bets.*

To be a winner at poker, you must hold your money dear and value it like gold. There are good bets in poker, and there are bad bets. If you can cut the number of your bad bets in half, right there, you will probably have turned the tide. You'll be turning losing sessions into winning sessions, and small winning sessions into larger winning sessions.

Never lose sight of this concept when you're playing. Do not play with cards that cannot win. This principle holds true at all points of the game in poker. When you lose, you should lose on hands you thought would be winners or which gave you good odds to play out as an underdog. Never lose on hands on which your odds of winning aren't worth the bets you're making, because you shouldn't even be playing them.

Folding when you're out of the running is precept number one if you're going to be a winning player. Folding bad hands will make you more money in the long run than any other type of strategy you can pursue. This thinking should not be interpreted as advice to play like a rock, or to exit pots just because your hand is a dog, or to bet only when you're in the lead. Far from it. Smart poker play is balancing bets with chances of winning, and that includes playing for pots when you're strong, when you're trailing, and sometimes when you're weak.

When you do play second best or worse hands, it should be because they give you good value—your long term expectation is to win money in that particular situation. You may be an underdog in a hand, but if, overall, playing this type of hand gives you more profits than losses, you should play it. Playing only good hands will mark you as predictable, and playing too many bad hands will bury you in losses. For the best result, you must strike a balance in between the two extremes.

How do you know when staying in a hand is a correct play? It's not always easy to figure out just what the right move is in a game, even with hindsight, but that's what makes poker so fascinating. Experience and study will get you in the right direction.

Your goal in poker must be to win money. Having

constant action and being part of every pot is a losing strategy. By definition, it means you're playing in too many pots, with too many inferior hands, for too long. This is not a winning strategy. At the least, you need to start with cards that can win. Let's look at that concept now.

WINNING CONCEPT #3: Play with Starting Cards that Can Win

Sometimes you're dealt playable starting cards; sometimes you're not. Obviously, in the first case, you'll play the playable hands and see where they take you as the deal goes on. But in the second instance, where your cards are not promising and you're a big underdog, the proper strategy is to fold.

Too many players start out a hand with weak cards that have little hope of improvement. They will initiate bets, call other player's bets, and even put themselves in situations where they can be raised and have to cough up yet another bet—all this in situations where their hand doesn't warrant a single bet in the first place!

The object in poker is to have the best hand at the showdown, which means that to win you must enter into the betting with hands that have a reasonable chance of winning. You won't win every hand you enter. If you did, there would rarely be any opponents contesting those pots. You must however, win enough money in the pots you do win to cover the losses from other pots you fall short in. To make this a mathematically sound pursuit, you need to bet, to some degree, in proportion to your winning chances. On a simplistic level, that means betting whenever you have a reasonable chance of winning, and folding when you don't.

The biggest mistake weak players make is to play too many hands. They're hypnotized by the action and don't want to miss any opportunities of catching a card that can make their hand a winner. Weak players will call bets and raises with inferior hands, endlessly waiting for a golden card that will take them down the yellow brick road. Now and again, underdog hands will draw out to win pots, but the wizard won't always be there, and that type of play will ultimately result in heavy losses. You have to avoid the temptation to play poor starting hands just for the sake of getting action. If you're playing to win, you must be selective in the cards you play.

WINNING CONCEPT #4: The Goal is to Win Money, Not Pots

There is a misconception among many players that winning more pots equates to being a bigger winner at the tables. In fact, the opposite is true! Weaker players tend to win more pots than stronger players because they're playing too many hands. Naturally, the more hands you play to the end, the more hands you will win, but that doesn't make for more profits. Every pot contested comes at a cost. When you contest many and lose many, it leads to a mighty bad day.

FIFTEEN CONCEPTS OF WINNING POKER

As the pros say, life is one long poker game. The goal is to win money, not pots. There is a significant difference between the two. After all, at the end of a poker session, you're not going to measure your results by how many pots you won. You probably won't even know the number. Neither will anyone else in the game. Nobody ever asks you how many pots you won, just simply, "Did you win?" Winning money is what counts in poker—the final result. And winning money should be your goal.

WINNING CONCEPT #5: Understand the Importance of Playing Position

Your position at the poker table is an important determinant in strategy decisions. Always consider how many players will act after your calls, bets, or raises, and how they might respond to your plays.

Players acting **under the gun**, that is, first, are in the weakest position. They not only have the least amount of information about how the opposing players are playing their hands, but they are also most vulnerable to raises and reraises. The result is that early position players must play a more conservative and cautious game. On the other hand, the player who acts last is in the best position. He gets a read of the entire table before acting on his hand, knows the action he is facing, and can adjust his strategy accordingly.

Players in the last position have leverage and flexibility. They can play a more aggressive game than early and middle position players. With the appropriate hands, last position players are in an excellent position to raise or bluff opponents out of the pot. Using their favorable positions, they can steal more antes than any other spot at the table. If the action is light, they have the luxury of watching all the preceding action and coming in cheaply without fear of a reraise, since their wagers will cap the betting for that round. If a bet and raise precedes the turn and they are facing a double bet with a marginal hand, it is easy to fold without cost.

> **The deeper the player's position is, the more playable a marginal hand is.**

On the other hand, a player holding a marginal hand in an early or middle position has no such choice. Perhaps he feels his hand is worth a bet, but certainly not two bets or more. The problem is that he cannot wait to see what happens. If a blind or bet precedes his position, forcing him to call or fold, and several or more opponents follow his position, he's in a vulnerable spot with a marginal hand. This position is susceptible to any of the succeeding players raising that bet, and even reraising.

If a marginal hand is worth just one bet, a player cannot take the chance of getting raised behind his position, and being whipsawed between several forces betting and raising each other. Thus, due to this vulnerable position, the correct play is to fold the marginal hand. Marginal hands are worth a play only at a marginal cost. The deeper the player's position is, the more playable a marginal hand is. As a general rule in borderline situations, go out with bad positioning and stay in with good positioning.

HELPFUL HINT

In dealer's choice games, the most advantageous games for the dealer to play are hold 'em, Omaha, and draw poker because of the special positional advantages the dealer holds in these games.

WINNING CONCEPT #6: Be Aware of the Pot Odds

Pot odds is a concept that looks at the risks against the rewards of making a bet—the risks being the cost of a bet, and the rewards being the amount of money to be won from the pot. For example, if the pot holds $100 and the bet to be called is $20, then the pot odds are $100 to $20, or 5 to 1. You use pot odds to determine if the cost of going for the pot is justified by the amount you might win. Let's look at an illustrative situation to see how this works.

Let's say you're playing $10-$20 seven-card stud and two opponents are left. You hold aces over 3s, and $40 is due your position. The first opponent, whom you figure for a probable three-of-a-kind, has opened on sixth street with a $20 bet. He was raised by the second player $20 more. The second player sits with four hearts and has straight possibilities as well, good scare cards against your two pair. With the $40 worth of bets, the pot now holds $240. According to the pot odds, should you call?

Of course, you don't know for sure what cards your opponents hold in the hole, but you figure your hand to be second best without improvement. You must draw an ace or a 3 to fill the two pair into a full house, the only way you can win the hand. However, the hearts hand has one of your 3s, and you noticed another 3 pass out of play earlier, leaving you, in fact, only two live cards, the remaining aces.

There has been a total of twenty-eight cards revealed: the eight open cards of your opponents, your six cards, and the fourteen cards folded earlier by the other players. That leaves twenty-four unknown cards. Only two of them, the aces, can help your hand. The odds of improving to be a winner are 2 in 24 (1 in 12), or 11 to 1 against. The pot offers only 6 to 1, poor odds against an 11 to 1 chance of improvement. Aces up is normally a powerful hand, but in this situation the correct play is to fold.

The above hand worked well as an illustration, because only one card was yet to be played, which made estimating your pot odds relatively easy. Estimating pot odds value with more than one card to play becomes more difficult as more unknowns come into play. How fast will the pot grow? What future bets will have to be called? What new cards dealt will change your projected strength vis-a-vis your opponents? Though more variables may come into play, and a pot odds analysis may become less exact, a rough cost-of-playing versus money-to-be-won calculation is always helpful in determining whether a hand is worth playing. Let's look at a pot odds application for draw poker.

Pot odds dictate that four-card straights and flushes should be folded before the draw if two other players or fewer are in the pot, unless the game is being played with a large ante. The chances of improving these four-card totals to a straight or flush are approximately 4 to 1 against. With less than three players in contention, the money in the pot is generally not enough to justify a call.

For example, in a $5-$10 poker game with eight participants and a $1 ante, the pot initially holds $8 worth of antes. If only one player calls the opener, these two $5 bets boost the pot up to $17 in bets and antes. With only $17 to win and a cost of $5 to call, the pot offers less than the 4 to 1 odds needed to make the call a good play. The smart move here is to fold.

On the other hand, if the above game were played with a high ante, say $2 per player, calling in the above situation would be an excellent play. The $10 in bets added to $16 in antes ($2 ante per player times eight players), fills the pot with $26 in bets and antes. Those are odds of 26 to 5 on the bet, better than the 4 to 1 odds needed to justify the call. Playing to the draw in this situation is an excellent move. While evaluating pot odds is not always an exact science, since you're making some estimations and there are always unknowns, it is a useful and important evaluation tool that will help you make profitable strategic decisions in poker.

WINNING CONCEPT #7: Learn to Read Tells and Watch Out for Your Own

There is a whole science in poker devoted to the art of reading "**tells,**" the inadvertant giving away of one's hand to opponents. Almost every player has tells, some better hidden than others. It is your job not only to seek out the tells from your opponents, but to protect against their finding yours.

There is a psychological and emotional reaction to every stimulus and event that occurs at a poker table, and a resultant physical expression of that reaction. The reaction can be expressed in some form of body language—like a player shifting in his seat, leaning forward, or scratching his head, or in a small facial expression like a twitch or tightening of the eyes, or perhaps as a faint grimace. The body is all movement—unless you're playing a carcass.

Learning to read tells is a master science. If you pay careful attention to the goings on at a poker table, you may occassionally be able to pick up signs that will clue you in to a player's hand or possible reaction to a situation. For example, some players lose interest every time they're about to fold. Others feign a loss of interest and appear distracted when they hold monster hands.

A typical tell in beginning games is a player grabbing his chips when he's going to call a bet, even though the action is several players in front of him. Another is a player who watches the action more closely when he knows that he will be participating in the betting. There are literally thousands of tells available for you to take advantage of—and guard against. Players may hold their cards differently or wear a different expression when they're going to fold. Other players can scarcely contain their excitement when they're dealt a big hand, and they may express this in all sorts of obvious mannerisms—*obvious*, that is, if you're paying attention.

Look for vocal patterns and tones, the playing of chips, the holding of cards, facial expressions, or where an opponent's eyes go (to his chip stack or an opponent's, to the pot subconsciously counting the money they hope to win, to other players' eyes, or at least to those of the one they fear most). Notice the way a player sits, whether he speaks more or less than normal, or louder or softer, or bets with more aggression (bluffing?) or more meekly, or tosses chips so that they barely make it into the pot (disguising strength?)

Stay alert and watch what's going on. The patterns will emerge. Finding and using these tells is worth lots of money to the astute player. Having prior information on a player's intentions or an actual tipping off of an opponent's strength or weakness after he makes a bet is, needless to say, a huge advantage in poker.

At the same time as you search out tells in your opponents, you must protect against their finding yours. Learn to develop a "poker face," so that when you've got the groceries, you can fill the bag.

WINNING CONCEPT #8: Disguise Your Betting Actions

Tells are not the only one way you can tip off your hand. Being predictable in your betting patterns is just as bad. If you're too consistent in your play, not only you will know what you're going to do, but so will your opponents!

Poker is a game of deceipt. Your actions—betting, calling, and raising are a process in disguising your hand and creating doubts in your opponents minds as to the relative strength of your hand. One of the worst things you can do as a poker player is become predictable. If your opponents know that you always bet, call, fold, and raise in the same situations, your play would be like an open book—and they would feast upon you at the table.

If, every time you bet or raise, more opponents than usual drop out of the action, something may be amiss. You must find that "something" to protect your pots. Whether it may be a tell or a predictable betting pattern, you have to fix your playing so you get the proper value for your bets.

If you're pegged as a player who plays only with good hands, or as one who raises every time a good hand is drawn, in no time at all, your opponents will pick up on this habit and adjust their play to take full advantage of the situation. For example, there are aggressive players who tip off good hands by suddenly playing meekly when their cards show strength. This unusual behavior often causes opponents to beware the quiet lion and drop out in marginal situations rather than meet the action.

To some degree, a good player *will* be predictable, and that is okay. There is always a degree of consistency in good players. But at the same time, unless you want to play like a complete nut so no one will ever know what you're doing—except losing—there has to be a certain degree of unpredictability in your play. Part of being a good poker player is varying your play enough so that opponents never know exactly what's up your sleeve.

WINNING CONCEPT #9: Strategy for Playing Against a Loose Player

Loose players love action. They will play too many hands, call too many bets, and stay in games too long. By playing more hands, they will win more pots, but at the expense of giving away too many bets when they finish out of the money.

Since loose players stay in pots with weaker hands, you can contest early pots against them with lesser hands than you normally would consider. In the late rounds, at the showdown, you'll call more often, since loose players will contest showdowns with weaker cards.

Don't bluff against a loose player. It's difficult to bluff him out of the pot. Overall, a good strategy to pursue against loose players is to stick to a fundamentally solid game, playing a little looser than normal, and playing aggressively only when you have the strength.

WINNING CONCEPT #10: Strategy for Playing Against Frequent Bluffers

Players who bluff often contribute a lot of money to pots. That's good, especially when you're sitting with a better hand than the bluffer. When you draw great hands, if the bluffer is in motion, you're in great shape and can play quietly while the pot is built up for you.

The general strategy against a freqeunt bluffer is to call his bets more often when you have a hand that can challenge and beat the bluffer's hand if he doesn't have the goods. You have two ways to beat the bluffer. First, you can win because you already have a better hand. Second, your hand can improve enough to be a winner. Before calling, you must make sure your hand is strong enough on its own merits to make a stand. It must at least have the potential to improve to be a winner if the opponent is not bluffing. Just because you know someone is bluffing doesn't mean you need to play for the pot. Your hand must stand on its own.

WINNING CONCEPT #11: Strategy Against Tight Players

You should play a looser game against a tight player, a player who makes and calls bets only when he holds good hands. Since this player won't play with mediocre cards, you can force him out of the pot early with strong bets. You'll be saving money whenever your hand is mediocre and he bets.

Take advantage of his tight play by always figuring him for a good hand when he's in the pot. Respect his bets; he's generally betting on solid situations. In borderline situations, give him the benefit of the doubt and call his bets less often. When you do call his bets, call with cards you figure can win, and if he raises, make sure the pot odds and the strength of your hand justify a call.

WINNING CONCEPT #12: Strategy Against Players Who Don't Bluff

When you're not sure, give the non-bluffer the benefit of the doubt and fold marginal hands. You save money against this type of player by calling less with questionable hands and by not having your good hands bluffed out by his scare cards. This type of player is predictable, and that gives you a big edge in poker.

WINNING CONCEPT #13: Learning to Improve Your Play

Becoming a more proficient poker player requires that you pay attention to your opponents' moves and mannerisms during the course of a poker game. Hands and situations repeat themselves over and over again in poker. The wise player benefits from these experiences and can apply the knowledge he gains to future hands.

While learning from mistakes is a great step in improving skills, a smart player also learns from his wins, and from other players' wins and losses. He also learns from mistakes and the strong plays made by opponents. Every deal is a poker class that can provide a lesson, large or small.

The improving poker player examines every situation and hand to see how it could have been played optimally. For example, on a lock-type hand, could an extra bet have been forced out of the losers, or could more players have been kept in the pot with a different betting pattern? Or on a hand that lost, could it have been played more aggressively so that opponents could have been forced out earlier? Should the player have bowed out earlier himself, realizing that maybe the winner's betting suggested a better hand than could be beat?

A lot of poker knowledge is learned by observing. Watch your opponents and see how they react to the different situations that come up in a poker game. The more you learn about your opponents, the better your chances of squeezing extra bets out of them, building bigger pots for yourself when the cards are right, and beating them more consistently.

How well you do in poker is not measured by the actual winning or losing of each hand, but by *how well you played that hand*. You must always examine your play and ask youself the question, "Did I play the cards optimally?" Just because you won a hand doesn't mean you played it well. Conversely, just because you lost a hand doesn't mean you played it poorly. Perhaps you could have won a bigger pot, or perhaps you should have forced out another player and gotten lucky when he didn't draw out on you. Maybe you stayed in one card too many. Maybe you shouldn't have played the hand at all.

If you constantly stay aware of how the game is being played and keep track of the tendencies of other players, you can't help becoming a better player. And playing better means winning more.

WINNING CONCEPT #14: Only the Best Hand Wins

Do not fall in love with your cards, no matter how pretty they look. There are no prizes for second best at poker. Only the winner takes the cake. If you have kings over 6s on Fifth Street in seven-card stud, and an opponent gets dealt an open pair of aces, the dirge has begun. If those aces are paired with a second pair, you're chasing with a dead hand.

Aces up beat kings up in poker. Though you may improve, those aces have an equal chance of improving. Unless you have very compelling pot odds, the romantic interlude is over—it's time to fold.

Sometimes you must fold strong hands in the face of heavy betting, even though you suspect an opponent is suspected of bluffing. There's nothing wrong with being bluffed out of pots. That's part of the game. If you are never bluffed out of a pot, that means you're calling too often, and opponents are reaping showdown harvest with this loose play. Good players respect cards and can be bluffed. Only weak players will never give up the ship—until it sinks. Don't worry about trying to scratch out a win in every pot. Just win the ones you can and minimize losses in the ones you can't.

WINNING CONCEPT #15: Be Smart With Money Management

There can never be enough said about how important money management is in the winning formula. From betting within one's means to minimizing losses and maximizing gains to emotional control, money management is the key to being a winner. Be sure to read the money mangement chapter carefully and follow its advice.

9. PERCEPTIONS AND PLAYERS

In this chapter we'll take a look at the human part of the game, the types of players you might face and the perceptions and counter-perceptions that influence the dynamics of a poker game. This is just a brief introduction to this aspect of poker, hopefully enough to get your mind flowing in the right direction.

THE GAME OF PERCEPTIONS

While many players evaluate the possibilities of what their opponents may hold judging by the cards they see and how they are betting, it is equally important to consider what cards your opponent thinks you hold. For example, while his play indicates types of hands he may have, so too does your play indicate some possibilities about what you may be holding. Poker, after all, is a game of logic and assessment. Intelligent players are always evaluating and reevaluating situations according to the actions of their opponents. While you are studying your opponents, they are studying you. What are you representing by your betting—a strong hand, a weak hand, a lock? Are you bluffing?

As you analyze what you think they think you have, their actions become more understandable, and you'll have more information to draw from in making your decisions. For example, in seven-card stud, if your first three open cards are spades, and you've been betting according to a pattern that would lend credence to a flush, you'll have a lot more information about an opponent when his aggressive opening betting gets much more tentative as the third flush card is revealed.

RELATIVE GAME HAND STRATEGY

Poker is a game of relative strengths. A lowly pair of sevens may take a pot in one hand, and a mighty full house may fall prey to a higher full house or even a four-of-a-kind in another. It is unlike video poker machines, where the schedule on the outside of the machines gives you an absolute payout for the poker hands you draw. In live table poker, what is one hand's rose, may be another's barren crop; it is all relative.

The beauty of poker is that while you never really know what opponents hold in the hole, you can make educated guesses based on the way they are betting from the particular position in which they sit. As we discussed earlier, position plays an important role in what hands a player can and cannot call, bet, or raise with. If you evaluate the cards you see, the betting patterns of the table, the positions and actions of the players, and the dynamics of the hand, you can make some reasonable deductions.

PERCEPTIONS AND PLAYERS

Players who bet strong in early positions, for example, are advertising strength. They'll need to weather possible raises after their position. In contrast, players who bet strong in late position against little opposition aren't necessarily playing the strength of their hands. They may just be playing the position.

Of course, while opponents come in a variety of strengths and dispositions, you can narrow them down to "types" and play them accordingly. You'll soon learn which opponents play aggressively and which won't budge with a bet unless they've got a strong hand, which ones stay too long in pots and which players bluff too often or not at all. All this goes into the cauldron of your knowledge to be used in every situation to understand just how strong or weak your hand is at that particular moment.

Bets, calls, and raises are made for particular reasons, and over time, you'll get a better sense of what those reasons are. For example, if two opponents are betting into your four-straight in seven-card stud, and you believe they think you have a straight, you need to factor that into your decision-making. To be successful at poker, you need to know when you're standing strong, when you're weak, when you're a virtual lock with the strength of your hand, and when your hand has possibilities but is trailing in strength to what you perceive your opponents are holding. Again, it's all a game of mutual perception.

Let's now take a look at the types of relative hands you might hold and the general strategy to pursue when you're playing these hands.

THE FOUR TYPES OF HANDS

You can define the types of hands you receive in poker into several categories, all of which are relative to the situation you're facing. At the top of these categories are the "lock," hands—holdings which are heavily favored to win the pot against all competition. At the bottom rung are the weak hands—holdings which are rarely worth a bet. In between, are the strong hands and the trailing hands, and that's the arena where most of your pots will be played.

In this section, we'll look at the four types of poker hands and the general strategies you would pursue with them. We'll start with the worst poker hand, the weak hand, and work our way up to the strongest grouping, the "lock."

WEAK HANDS

This category describes hands with no better than longshot chances of improving to be a winner. These are the worst poker hands, and they have long-term losing expectations. The best strategy is to get out once there is a cost to playing the hands.

Weak Hand Strategy

Weak hands should be junked at the first opportunity. When you're a heavy underdog with little hopes of winning, you have no business investing your money in the pot. You must fold your cards immediately. This advice applies to your starting cards, and it applies to your cards at any point in the game that they become weak. It doesn't matter how promising the career of your beloved cards was when you began. Losing hands are losing hands. If you have trip kings and an opponent shows trip aces on board, you're beaten, baby. Your kings might as well be marshmallows in a rock fight. They're not going to do you any good.

Too many players chase pots with weak hands, hoping for the lucky draw. That kind of strategy is costly and leads to consistent losing sessions. To be an overall winner at poker, you must avoid throwing away money on poor percentage plays. Every bet you save makes your bankroll that much richer.

TRAILING HANDS

One step above the weak hand scenario is the trailing hand. You do not figure to currently have the best hand, nor are you favored to win if the hand is played out. Of course, a good draw will change that designation rapidly, but at the moment, you don't figure to have a strong enough hand to be considered a favorite or near-favorite. You need to improve.

Trailing Hand Strategy

Relatively speaking, a trailing hand is an underdog. Under the right circumstances, though, it does have some redeeming value. If the trailing hand can get into a pot cheaply or even grab a **free card**—allow a player to proceed to the next round for free because all players have checked—then this type of hand is worth playing to the next card. When the cost is a stiff bet, however, trailing hands must be folded and thrown to the wind. The winning possibilities of borderline hands aren't strong enough to warrant heavy investments into a pot.

A pair of jacks (J J), for example, is a marginal starting hand at hold 'em. It holds some possibilities of becoming a strong hand with a favorable flop, but at the cost of weighty betting, or the threat of having to meet raises behind its position, this hand isn't worth a call. If an ace, king, or queen appears on the flop, the jacks begin to pale under the bright lights. A pair of jacks are heavy underdogs to the probable queens, kings, or aces of opponents. If they are played against a flop like this, they will, in the long run, take heavy losses.

Position also plays an important role in the play of a trailing hand. From the last position, you can play a trailing hand because there is no possibility of being raised. In early position, though, a call would be fraught with the danger of a possible raise after the position. This is not a situation you want with a trailing hand.

To sum up, trailing hands are worth a play when the price is right, but if the cost is at a premium, they're rarely worth betting on. Save your sweet dreams for the late night, after the poker game. And save your money as well.

STRONG HANDS

This category represents cards which have excellent possibilities of improving into winners, and in fact are favorites or near-favorites, but can in no way be considered lock hands. The starting hand A K in hold 'em, for example, is a strong hand with excellent winning potential. If all players stay in for the flop, though, the A K is subject to all sorts of flops which could make it an underdog.

Strong Hand Strategy

With strong hands, play aggressively. These types of hands have a good head start, but if you don't raise and force some players out, you take the risk of allowing mediocre hands to draw out and beat you. The more players in the pot, the higher the average winning hand will be and the higher the chance that a strong hand will turn into second best.

Let's illustrate this with an example. Suppose five players all have a chance at winning, and given your starting cards, you have three of those chances. Each of the remaining players has one chance each. Together, of those seven winning chances, you hold only three of them. This makes you an underdog to win the pot even though individually, you have the best chances of any one player. But if you were able to force out two of those opponents, of the five total chances of winning, you would now have shifted the odds in your favor, having three of the five total chances (instead of seven).

This simple example is not that far from the truth. The more weak hands you allow in to see a card, the greater the chances are that one of those weaker hands will improve and become a better hand than yours. By playing weakly with a strong hand, you increase the competition and decrease the chances of your strong hand finishing on top.

With strong hands, play aggressively right from the start. Either force out the marginal and weak hands or build up a pot which you're favored to win. With a strong but non-lock hand, you never should allow marginal or weak hands to play cheaply. If opponents want to see the show, they'll have to buy the tickets—at the price of your bets and raises.

If your previously strong hand appears now to be second best to a better hand, downgrade its relative value. *It is no longer strong.* The strong hand, by definition, means you're leading the pack. When that hand weakens to a trailing strength, you need to reevaluate it according to the new situation.

It is important to adjust strategies according to the situation. Poker is not a game of rigid corrects and incorrects. You must be able to think on your feet, using your skills and instincts in the context of smart poker play. To sum up: when you've got a good hand, you need to protect it by weeding out the competition so your hand has the best chance of taking the pot.

LOCK HANDS

Lock hands put you in the driver's seat in poker. You figure to have a win, and you want to build up the pot as much as possible. There are two types of lock hands: the exposed ones in stud games (where the strength of your hand is apparent or suggested to all opponents) and the hidden ones (where other players have no idea of the strength of your hand).

For example, if you have three kings in the hole in seven-card stud, and K 8 7 6 as upcards, you're sitting with a monster hand that no opponent can see or perhaps even guess at. The strength is hidden. On the other hand, if three of those kings are on board, there is strength exposed for all to see. Only an opponent who thinks they can beat your represented hand, or the possibility of a kings up full house or better would dare play for a nickel more. Note that I'm using the concept of the "lock" as the strongest relative position in poker, one that is a huge favorite to win except against the most uncanny luck by an opponent.

Lock Hand Strategy

Having a lock hand puts you in a powerful position. Your only strategic concern is to get as much of your opponents' money in the pot as possible. In one ideal situation, other players will have been dealt strong hands as well—though not as strong as yours, of course—and they'll be bidding up the pot. In another ideal scenario, modest betting by many opponents will make the pot interesting and let players stay for more bets in hopes of improving.

Even though you would love to raise and reraise until your opponents' pockets are emptied, on a practical level, overzealous betting will drive your opponents out of the pot, and that is exactly what you don't want to do. On the other hand, overly timid betting, if it's not your style for the situation, may very well clue your opponents in that you've got the goods and are sandbagging them.

So you must strike a balance, gauging the situation for the way to keep the most players interested. You need them to contribute to a pot that will be yours at the showdown.

UNDERSTANDING LEVELS OF PLAY

Of course there are many levels and degrees of skill and aggressiveness among players, but to a great degree, skill levels can be grouped into several general categories. We'll take a brief look at each.

BEGINNING/WEAK PLAYERS

Beginning and weak players often share one tendency in common: they play too many hands and stay in pots too long. They place bet after bet into pots they shouldn't be playing because they don't recognize that they are not getting enough value for their wagers. You'll see this type of behavior over and over again among weaker players. In this category, you can also find the **rock**—the tight player who will play only with good cards. The rock's play is so obvious that all opponents without strong enough hands fold at the very first sign of his activity. But even more prevalent than the rock are the legions of loose gooses, the players who spread money around the pot like it's going out of style.

Weaker players are weaker players for many other reasons as well, but their prevailing feature is that they play too many hands for too long. They'll win more pots than the average player, but at such cost that anything less than really good luck will probably spell losses for their session.

AVERAGE PLAYERS

Average players will also make too many bets, but not as many as the weak players. They will play a more solid game. But they are average players for other reasons as well. Besides contributing too much money to other people's pots (where instead they should be watching from the sidelines), they don't maximize the wins from their good hands. They drop out of hands they should still be playing. They have some basic abilities in reading the table, but they can't compete with better players, who will eat them for lunch.

Average players play good hands too weakly and allow opponents to draw free cards, thus allowing too many hands to draw out on them. When an average player's hand is relatively strong, he'll call when the action comes his way, allowing players behind his position to come in for just one bet. A strong player in that situation would raise to thin the competition. Among average players there will still be some rocks and gooses, but they'll have some more skills than their more novice counterparts.

STRONG PLAYERS

What separates the average players from the *strong players* will soon be apparent at a poker game. The characteristic quality of a strong player is aggressive betting. Unlike average players, who will frequently call—the type of bettor pros term **calling stations**—strong players will sooner raise than call. You'll rarely get a free card out of them. Action will be fiercer, and you'll soon know the meaning of having to "pay to play." Strong players instill fear in their opponents at a table and leverage every bet to the maximum effectiveness. When the situation is right, they'll punish opponents who have the temerity to bet into their position. Strong players know how to read and drive the action at the table. They're tough players, and they make opponents earn every dime that they win against them.

THE VERY BEST

The very best poker players excel in every aspect of the game. They're super aggressive, and they have no fear of any bet thrown their way. They also have the uncanny ability to read opponents based on the action and play of the table, and this talent allows them to play poker at a championship level.

10. BLUFFING

The bluff! The beauty, romance, and drama of poker lies in the bluff. It's an integral part of poker and an art that matures with experience. There are several advantages to bluffing. The first and most obvious advantage is that you can "steal pots" from better hands and win money you otherwise would not have seen. There is nothing more beautiful than chasing out a better hand and taking the pot for your own.

Players who are known not to bluff will, on average, win smaller pots than players who are known to bluff.

The second advantage to bluffing is that when you're caught, you have put doubt in your opponents' minds. They will suspect you for possible garbage every time you contest the pot. This powerful weapon makes your play more difficult to predict, and it will win you bigger pots when you do have strong hands. Players with weaker hands will feel compelled to call your position more often thinking that their hands may be better. While they are keeping you "honest," your winning pot sizes get larger.

Predictable play is costly in poker, whether in the home game, casino game, or club game. Players who are known not to bluff will, on average, win smaller pots than players who are known to bluff. That is a fact. Opponents with mediocre hands will know that it is senseless to compete against the rock, because the rock only plays strong hands. On one hand, players are saving a bundle by folding with hands that likely won't come in first, on the other hand, the rock is not getting as much value on his good hands as he should.

To be successful at poker, you must make bluffing an integral part of your game. You'll not only win pots where your hand is not the best one, you'll also win larger pots because opponents will contest your winning hands more often. There's no exact formula for successfully bluffing at poker. Each game is its own ball of wax, tied up in the unique dynamics of the game itself, the psychology of the setting, the venue where it's played, and the players comprising the game.

Let's go over some important bluffing concepts.

BLUFFING

TEN POINTERS ON BLUFFING

1. BLUFFING IN LOW LIMIT GAMES

In many low limit games, players simply cannot be chased from a pot. For one thing, the action is cheap, and the thinking goes, "What's one or two more bets?" For another thing, low limit games attract players who can't be chased out of a pot with anything short of an elephant stampede. They'll call bet after bet with terrible hands in losing situations and hope for the longshot draw that just might give them the winner. They get those cards now and then, but in between, they get bled unmercifully.

If you're in a low limit game where players are not getting chased out of pots with maximum bets, there's no point in bluffing. If you can't bluff out an opponent, you need to redirect your strategy toward more basic play, working the cards a little more than working the opponents.

Some players claim that you can't ever bluff players out of the pot in low limit games. That's certainly true for some games, but not for all. You'll find low limit casino games, say $1-$3, where players respect bets and can be bluffed. After all, to many people, money is money. The stakes may be small, but they would sooner save their bets for situations with better prospects. However, as each game has its own mix of players and particular temperament, you'll see what can and can't be done on a game by game basis.

2. BLUFFING IN MEDIUM-HIGH LIMIT GAMES

Unlike in a low stakes casino game, a bluff in medium to high limit games may register from the opening bell right down to the final round. With more money at stake, players are less subject to the "friendly game syndrome" of staying in the pot a few rounds. They may immediately fold if the betting is too large for the value of their hand.

In casino and club poker games, a rule of thumb is that the higher the stakes, the better the level of player. As you play in higher stake games, your effectiveness in chasing opponents out of the pot will improve. The simple fact is that good players respect situational betting and can be bluffed.

Of course, you have to pick your spots. Every game has its mix of strong and weak players, and you'll need to learn as the game goes on who you can bluff, and who just won't understand he should be exiting the action. Poor players don't see the table well and, as we discussed earlier, don't realize that their hands can't support the action there. Players who cannot be bluffed are players who play too many pots. If you find opponents like that in your game, that's good anyway.

3. SMALL POT VS. LARGE POT BLUFFING

In limit poker, bluffing is more effective in smaller pots than in large pots for the simple reason that, in large pots, there is simply too much money at stake for players to fold against the cost of a few more bets. With good pot odds and a lot of money at stake, it is hard to force savvy players from the sweet corn in the fields.

If an opponent is looking at a 1 in 3 chance of winning, and a bet to play would cost but 1/15 of the pot, it would be foolish not to play with such good odds. Of course, bluffing opportunities may present themselves in any type of situation. Generally speaking, though, bluffs are much more effective in small pots for the reason given above.

With small pots, on the other hand, the thinking is the opposite: opponents will feel it is not worth playing for a small pot at the cost of a big bet unless they either think they have you beat with what you may be representing, they have good pot odds, or they don't buy your representation of a strong hand. Otherwise, the pot odds simply aren't favorable to challenge for the pot with an inferior hand.

4. BLUFF THE RIGHT PLAYER

It's easier to bluff a good player than a weak one, and it's smarter to bluff a player who will likely bow out than one who won't. It's simply percentages. When targeting a bluff, choose situations that give you the best opportunity of success. It's common sense, but still worth stating.

Many players seem to bluff indiscriminately; apparently they don't care about their target. That is a mistake. If you get a good scare card, say an ace, don't try to power out an opponent who will likely call anyway. There is no sense trying to bluff a player who won't be bluffed, unless you want to increase the pot for other reasons. Always choose your situations with potential success in mind.

5. AVOID MULTI-PLAYER BLUFFS

Bluffs are most effective against just one opponent. You may even be able to bluff two players. The more players in the pot, however, the greater the chances are that at least one player will call the bet. With three or more players in the pot, there are too many possibilities for the bluff to fail. First, you now need to fool too many players. Second, perhaps one of those players you're trying to fool just has too strong a hand to go out with. Every time you add an additional opponent into the mix, the chances of that bluff's working go down considerably, and your bluff, simply by the law of averages, is much less likely to work. Avoid bluffing when more than two players remain in the game.

6. TIME YOUR BLUFFS

Pick your spots carefully. Bluffing is a matter of timing and circumstance. When done judiciously, bluffing will make you a stronger player and a bigger winner. Bluffing too frequently can get expensive. As opponents tend to believe you less and call you more, your inferior hands will be taking extra betting losses. That's not good for the bankroll.

7. BLUFF AGAINST SCARED PLAYERS

Watch for players who are losing heavily or have lost heavily and regained some of their losses. Psychologically, you have them in a position where they are more easily intimidated by your betting than normal. Players on a downward roll tend to play scared. They are more easily bluffed when they don't have the goods. The more players worry over their winnings or losses, the more leverage you have to push them around with aggressive betting. Players who play timidly are also easily bluffed and bullied out of pots you can collect for yourself. They make for great targets.

8. BLUFF ON THE ROLL

When you're on a roll, and winners seem to follow winners, bluffing becomes a more effective weapon in your game. When you've got the fear factor going in a game, it's a great time to ride that momentum with well-timed bluffs. Players are intimidated by the hot hand and respect bets more than they would otherwise.

9. OVERBLUFFING

It is one thing to bluff on occassion; it is another to bluff constantly. "Overbluffing" will drain you quickly, as opponents quickly catch on to your ways. Bluffing is most effective in small doses. Overbluffing is another way to say "playing too loosely,"—otherwise known as "betting too much," and consequently losing too much.

10. FRIENDLY GAME SYNDROME

Many poker games, particularly home affairs and low-limit casino and club games, tend to be more friendly than competitive. Players stay in more pots and play deeper into the hands. In situations like these, where players want to see more cards before folding and the play is loose, it is difficult to bluff opponents out in the early part of the deal. Often, your attempts at bluffing will be fruitless, and it would be better to play a straight game.

Further into the deal, however, the "sociable" players will begin to bow out as they realize that their longshots are no longer worth pursuing, especially when the larger bets start hitting the pot.

11. CLUB AND CASINO POKER

Playing poker in clubs or casinos is different than playing in your regular Friday night game. The players and level of play tend to be more competitive, and there is usually a stricter bet and rule structure. While many players are there for fun, at the same time, there is a greater emphasis on winning.

In addition to tourists and local players, you'll often find local professionals grinding out a living at games of $5-$10 and higher. As opposed to your buddies back home in the Friday night game, players at these games are a lot less concerned about how your week went and a lot more interested in whatever green you're flashing that they hope to move into their own stack. The play of low-level pros at $5-$10 may not be spectacular, but it will be steady, and the overall competition will be better than you may be used to. As you move up the money tree, as we discussed earlier, you'll be running with bigger wolves.

Playing against local pros at smaller stake games doesn't mean you can't win money. First of all, if you're a decent player yourself, you may be equal to or better than the local pros. Second, there are always suckers at every game, patsies who never seem to learn a thing and are consistent losers contributing to everybody's pots.

I've emphasized lower stakes games thus far for a reason; the level of money being wagered in a poker game has everything to do with the level of competition you'll be playing against, and thus your chances of winning. The larger the stakes, the better the players. Pros playing in the $5-$10 game compete there because they're not good enough, gutsy enough, or well-financed enough to play at say, the $15-$30 game. The same applies for the $15-$30 and higher games. If the players could afford to profitably play for bigger stakes, they would move up to the bigger fish pond.

In casino and club poker, you're not playing against the casino. You're playing against other players, and that's where the money your wager has everything to do with your chances of winning. Let's look at this more closely.

CLUB AND CASINO POKER STRATEGY

A simple fact you must face in clubs and casinos is that the higher the stake of the game, the higher the level of competition. In a higher stakes game, the tourists and local players tend to be better (though there seems to be poor players at most levels of play), and most definitely, the pros are better. Pros that squeeze out their living at $5-$10 will get picked clean at $15-$30, while $15-$30 players will get chewed up and spit out at $30-$60.

If a pro could earn money at a higher level game, he certainly would. He's playing to make as much money as possible and there's more money to be had with bigger stakes. You can measure a pro's skills by the betting level of game he plays.

As a poker player, no matter how small or large your bankroll, you must be aware of your skill level compared to the level of game being played. For example, if you're a fairly decent player, you may be able to compete with the tourists and local pros at the $5-$10 game. At the $15-$30 game, however, the competition may eat you for breakfast. Your risk factor at higher stakes tables increases for far more than the obvious money management reasons—it increases because you're facing better players.

POKER IN THE U.S. AND CANADA

Club poker can be found everywhere in the United States and Canada: either legally—as in many states; openly tolerated, though not exactly legal—as in some locales; or simply underground—as in other places where open poker is not permitted by law.

In recent years, legalized gambling has spread like wildfire. States are finding that gambling tax revenues are a great source of income, especially in these hard times where governments are pressed for tax dollars. And, they figure, poker games are being played anyway. Why not legalize poker and get a piece of the action?

Deadwood, South Dakota put themselves on the map and revitalized their entire area with the approval of gaming in their town. Bringing back the spirit of the Wild West, this old frontier town legalized poker as well as other casino games. It now boasts a booming economy. Wild Bill Hickok's last poker game was played in Deadwood, and the hand he held when he was shot dead at the table, aces and 8s, is the most legendary poker hand of all. In poker parlance today, aces and 8s is known as "The Dead Man's Hand."

Dead Man's Hand

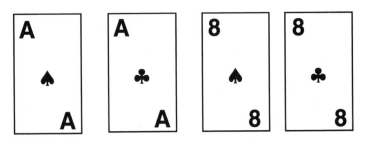

Legal poker is especially big in the West. Besides in Nevada and California, the two biggest legal poker playing states, legal poker clubs now exist in many other states around the country, as well as in parts of Canada.

Many of these clubs offer discounts on buy-ins to

help attract new players to the games. For example, on a minimum buy-in of $20, a club may give a new player $30 or even $40 in chips. That's quite a nice incentive. In return, the player must play a minimum amount of time or return the premium. If a player **busts-out** (loses his table stake), there is no penalty.

Poker clubs make their money either by charging each player a half-hourly or hourly fee for the seat, or, as in Vegas, with a **rake**—a percentage of money taken out of the pot by the dealer as the house cut. Poker clubs vary from the simple one game joints to opulent multi-game operations, where the player will find fine dining, restaurants, a full-service bar, and even live music.

Poker is not limited to the West. Indian casinos are springing up around the country. They offer good poker games as well. These venues give poker players, in addition to home games, plus legal, semilegal, and illegal card rooms, ample opportunity to test their skills at poker pretty much wherever they live.

Wherever you decide to test your skills, keep your mind focused on winning. That's what the game is all about. Be a winner!

12. MONEY MANAGEMENT

To be a winner at poker, you must exercise sound money management principles and have emotional control. The temptation to ride a winning streak too hard in the hopes of a big killing or to bet wildly during a losing streak, trying for a quick comeback, are the most common factors that destroy gamblers. Inevitably, the big winning sessions dissipate into small wins or disastrous setbacks, while moderately bad losing sessions can turn into nightmares.

In any gambling pursuit, where luck plays a role, fluctuations in one's fortunes are common. It is the ability of a player to successfully deal with these pendulous swings of the bankroll that is a vital element in the winning formula. Luck certainly plays a role in what cards are drawn, and, in the short run, can sway its weight toward or against player. The overriding factor in poker, though, is skill. It is the play of those cards received that determines the end result.

Good players don't always win, just as poor players don't always lose. That's a fact of life at the poker tables. You can't win every hand or every session. However, if you stick by the winning principles outlined in this book and follow the money management advice outlined in this section, you should end up a consistent winner at poker.

The player that consistently gives his winnings back to the table doesn't give himself a chance to win. In a sense, he's a player who *refuses* to win. No matter how well a poker session is going, that player feels the need to keep playing until the money is gone. He either subconsciously takes on losing habits or plays beyond the timeframe where he has the winning edge.

This player I'm describing is a loser, not a winner. He's not playing with the percentages. This type of bettor plays as if the goal were to lose. If he can't lose today, there's always tomorrow. For players hell-bent on losing, it doesn't take long for the losses to catch up with them. We've all seen it happen time and time again.

But losing is not what this book is about. It's about winning, and that's where I want your focus to be. What I'm trying to teach you here is how to win. Part of this formula is to use the winning techniques and strategies I describe throughout this book. Another part— the most important part—is to manage your money properly. If you don't handle your money intelligently and with a good plan from the start, you're going to be a loser at gambling.

How you feel most definitely affects your overall

chances of winning. There's no question about that. A player who goes into a game with the goal of winning does everything he can to achieve that goal. This gambler will closely follow the money management advice in this section. That's the mark of a winner. He'll play within his means, set reasonable limits, and control himself at the table. When he's winning big, he'll make sure a good chunk of that money stays with him.

Smart money management requires you to have a bankroll large enough to withstand the normal fluctuations of a poker game and to play for stakes within your financial and emotional means. In a sense, you must be street smart. There's no worse mistake than playing with money that you need for rent, food, or other living expenses. Your constant fear of losing that money will affect your play and influence you to make decisions that run contrary to sound poker principles. This brings us to the most important gambling dictum.

> *Never gamble with money you*
> *cannot afford to lose,*
> *either financially or emotionally.*

This caveat cannot be emphasized enough. Gambling with funds you need is a foolish play. Gambling involves chance, and the short term possibilities of taking a loss are real, no matter how easy the game may appear to be and no matter how stacked the odds are. Crazy things happen in gambling; that's what it's all about. If you never play over your head, you'll never suffer.

Find a game with stakes that make you comfortable, a game where the betting range fits your temperament and emotional makeup. If the larger bets of the particular game you're playing make your heart pump too hard, you're over your head. You need to find a game offering lower betting limits.

When you play with "scared money," you're easily bullied and pushed away from your optimum playing style. To win, you must go into the action with an edge and every emotional asset you have. You must not give your opponents the chance to push you around because the stakes are too dear for you. They'll figure that out quickly, and you'll be at a heavy disadvantage.

Remember that poker is a form of entertainment. As such, you must keep it in perspective. If the fear of losing money creates undue anxiety in you, the entertainment value (and probably your winning expectation) will slip rapidly. It's time to take a breather. Recoup your confidence; then hit the tables with fresh vigor. Play only with that winning feeling. Recognizing that emotions affect the quality of play is an important step in making poker an enjoyable and profitable experience.

BANKROLLING
As a rule of thumb, you'll need fifteen times the

maximum bet in a limit game for a sufficient table stake. For example, if you're playing a $5-$10 game, buy in for $150 (15 times $10). Similarly, at a $1-$3 table, spend $45 (15 times $3). For a $10-$20 game, bring $300 (15 times $20) to the table.

What often separates the winners from the losers in that the winners, when ahead, leave the table as winners. When they're losing, they restrict their losses to affordable amounts. Smart players never allow themselves to be wiped out in one session. It is important to limit your single session table stake to the limits mentioned above. If you do not dig in for more money, you can never be a big loser. As the saying goes, the first loss is the cheapest. You can't always win, so catch some fresh air. Play again when you're fresh and brimming with confidence.

KNOWING WHEN TO QUIT

Part of the successful money management formula is knowing when to quit. You won't always be at the top of your game. You may be exhausted after hours of play, annoyed with another player, or simply frustrated by bad hands. Whatever the case may be, the important thing to realize is that you're distracted, and the loss of concentration will hurt your play. It's time to take a break.

You might even find yourself in a game where everything's going your way. You're winning big, but you're getting tired. You feel like a superior player, but you've started making mistakes. You hate to leave such a choice table. What should you do?

Leave. Once you start making mistakes, you lose your edge. You might start handing back your winnings. Of course, it's tough to leave a game you feel is ripe for your skills, but when the edge is gone, it's gone. Take your winnings home with you.

MAXIMIZE WINS/MINIMIZE LOSSES

If you play poker regularly and your goal is win money on a consistent basis, you must not see every session as an end in itself and try to force wins when they just may not be there. Again, you can't win every time. During the times you lose, restrict your losses to a reasonable amount. You can't win every session, but if you're good, you can win most of them. Just as it's important to maximize your winnings at every winning session, it's equally important to minimize your losses at the losing ones.

Five Money Management Principles

1. Have a *winning attitude*. To win, you have to *want to be a winner.*

2. *Play within your means.*

3. *Protect your winning streaks*. Restricting losses is important; protecting your wins is equally important.

4. Have *emotional control*. Be in control of your situation, playing smart and coolly at all times—or leave.

5. Finally, *set limits*. Never allow yourself to take such a beating at poker that not only is your day or vacation ruined, but you've lost more money than you can afford. Any time that happens, it's always a disaster.

13. GLOSSARY

Ace: The card with one spot. The highest ranking card in high poker; in lowball, the lowest and therefore most valuable card.

Action: Betting.

Active Player: Player still in competition for the pot.

Ante: Uniform bet placed into the pot by players before the cards are dealt.

Ante-up: A call for a player or players to put their antes into the pot.

Bet: A unit of money wagered and placed into the pot.

Bicycle: In lowball, the A 2 3 4 5—the best possible hand. Also called the **Wheel**.

Blind: A mandatory bet that must be made on the first round of betting. Also, the player making that bet.

Blind Bet: The blind bet itself. Also, a bet placed without looking at one's cards.

Bluff: The act of betting heavily on an inferior hand for the purpose of intimidating opponents into folding their cards and making the bluffer a winner by default.

Bonus: Optional rule where a set amount is paid by all players to any holder of a high ranking hand such as a straight flush or a royal flush. Also called a **Royalty**.

Button: A marker used in casino games to indicate the dealer's position.

Buy-In: A player's investment of chips in a poker game or the actual amount of cash he uses to "buy" chips for play.

Call: To bet an amount equal to a previous bet on a current round of betting. Also known as **Calling a Bet** or **Seeing a Bet**.

Check: The act of "not betting" and passing the bet option to the next player while still remaining an active player. Players cannot check when a bet has been made. Also called **Pass**.

Check and Raise: A player's raising of a bet after already checking in that round. Usually not permitted in private games.

Cut: The amount of money taken from the pot by the house as its fee for running the game. The cut is also called **House Cut**, **Vigorish,** and the **Rake**. The cut is also the act of separating the cards into two piles and restacking them in reverse order.

Dealer: The player or casino employee who shuffles the cards and deals them to the players.

Dealer's Choice: A rule where the current dealer chooses the poker variation to be played.

Deuce: A card term for the 2 of any suit.

GLOSSARY

Down: A card dealt with its pips "face-down" so that its value is known only to the holder of the card. Cards that are dealt face-down are called **Downcards**, or **Closed Cards**.

Draw: The exchange of cards allowed after the first round of betting in draw poker variations.
Draw Out: The evolution of an inferior hand into a good one by the drawing of advantageous cards.

Draw Poker: A form of poker where all cards are dealt "closed," and seen only by their holder.

Face: The side of a card exposing its value.

Face-Down: When the side of a card identifying its value faces the table and is therefore hidden from public view. Only the holder of that card knows its value. Cards dealt face-down to the players are also known as **Downcards** or **Closed Cards**.

Face-Up: When the side of a card identifying its value is exposed and can be viewed by all players. Cards dealt face-up are also called **Open Cards**.

Fifth Street: The fifth card received in seven-card stud; the last round of betting in hold 'em and Omaha.

Flop: In hold 'em and Omaha, the first three cards simultaneously dealt face-up for communal use by all active players.

Flush: A hand of five cards of the same suit.

Fold: The withdrawal of further play in a hand. Also referred to as **Going Out**.

Four-Flush: A hand of four cards of the same suit.

Four-of-a-kind: A hand containing four cards of identical value, such as K K K K (four kings).

Four-Straight: A hand containing four cards in numerical sequence, such as 7 8 9 10.

Fourth Street: Fourth card dealt in seven-card stud; fourth community card exposed in hold 'em.

Free Card: A betting round where all players checked, thereby allowing players to proceed to the next round of play without cost. Also called a **Free Ride**.

Full House: A hand consisting of three-of-a-kind and a pair, such as 7 7 7 K K.

Hand: The cards a player holds; the best five cards a player can present.

Head to Head: Poker played by two players only —one against the other.

High Poker: Poker variations where the high hand wins.

Hole Card: Card held by a player whose value is hidden from other players.

Joker: The "53rd" card in a deck bearing the drawing of a joker or clown; sometimes used as a wild card.

Limit Poker: Poker in which the maximum bet size is set at fixed amounts. Limit poker is generally, though not necessarily, set up in a two-tiered structure, such as $5-$10.

Low Poker: A form of poker in which the lowest hand wins.

Misdeal: A deal deemed illegal and therefore invalid.

No Limit: Poker in which the maximum bet allowed is limited only by the amount of money the bettor has on the table.

Opener: The player making the first bet in a betting round; the bet itself.

Openers: In jacks or better, hands that can open the betting (consisting of a pair of jacks or higher ranking hands).

Pass: See **Check**.

Pat Hand: In draw poker, a hand to which no cards are drawn; also implies an excellent hand.

Picture Card: The jack, queen, or king.

Position: A player's relative position to the player acting first in a poker round.

Pot: The sum total of all antes and bets placed in the center of the table by players during a poker hand and collected by the winner or winners of that hand.

Pot Limit: A rule signifying that the amount of the largest bet can be no more than the current size of the pot.

Pot Odds: A concept which examines the cost of a bet against the money to be made by winning the pot and compares this to a player's chances of winning that pot.

Raise: A bet which equals a bet made previously in the round, plus an additional bet.

Rake: The amount of money taking out of the pot by the house as its fee for running the game.

Re-raise: A bet equaling a previous bet and raise, plus an additional bet—a raise of a raise.

Rough: In lowball, backing cards that are relatively high, such as 8 7 5 4 3, a rough 8.

Round: The complete cycle of checks, bets, folds, and raises occurring after each new card or cards are dealt; the complete cycle of cards dealt previous to or subsequent to betting.

Royal Flush: An A K Q J 10 of the same suit. The highest ranking hand in high poker.

Showdown: The final act of a poker game, where remaining players reveal their hands to determine the winner of the pot.

Seventh Street: The seventh and final card dealt in seven-card stud.

Sixth Street: The sixth card dealt in seven-card stud.

Smooth: In lowball, backing cards that are relatively low, such as 8 4 3 2 A, a smooth 8.

Stand Pat: In draw poker, to draw no cards.

Straight: A sequence of five consecutive cards of mixed suits, such as 4 5 6 7 8.

GLOSSARY

Straight Flush: A sequence of five consecutive cards in the same suit, such as 8 9 10 J Q of spades.

Stud Poker: Variation of poker where one or more cards are visible to the other players.

Suited: Cards of the same suit.

Table Stakes: A rule stating that a player's bet or call of a bet is limited to the amount of money he has on the table in front of him.

Tell: An inadvertent mannerism or reaction that reveals information about a player's hand.

Third Street: The first round of betting in seven-card stud.

Trips: Three-of-a-kind.

Two-Way Hand: A hand that can be played for both high and low.

Under the Gun: The first player to act in a round of poker.

Up: A card dealt with its pips "face up" so that its value can be viewed by all players. Cards that are dealt face up are called **Upcards**.

Wild Cards: Cards designated as "wild" can be given any value, even as a duplicate of a card already held, by the holder of that card.

FREE ONLINE GAMBLING MAGAZINE
www.cardozacity.com

Super Gambling Mega-Site and Magazine

Check out Cardoza Publishing's new online gambling magazine. We feature a content-rich publication targeted to you, loaded with articles, columns, how-to information, and so much more: everything you need to know about the world of gambling is presented to you at Cardoza City.

We'll keep you coming back with great articles and strategy advice on the games you play (blackjack, craps, slots, video poker, roulette, poker, more!), the sports you follow and bet on (baseball, football, boxing, basketball), and the stranger-than-fiction gambling stories that are just so fascinating, crazy, and, well, so true-to-life you will hardly believe it! There is everything here you want: articles on the world of internet gambling, the Book Corner- featuring new book reviews, the Vegas View- loaded with up-to-date listings on hotels, restaurants, casinos, and the sites & sounds of Sin City. Participate in our Beautiful Model and Crazy Fan of-the-month contests, check out the tip of the week, sign up for Avery Cardoza's online gambling school, and so much more...Wow!

We'll give you the confidence Cardoza Publishing puts behind every word in print. And no one knows more about gambling than Cardoza Publishing, seller of more than 6,500,000 books and the world's foremost publisher of games and gambling literature. Our writers are the real deal, many of them million-selling book authors who write exclusively under the Cardoza banner – try finding these legends and authorities on any other site.

Get ready for an esteemed website from the real world of publishing, featuring great content, class, authoritative writing, and the best winning tips on the world of gambling: Cardoza City!

come visit us now!
www.cardozacity.com

CARDOZA SCHOOL OF BLACKJACK
- Home Instruction Course - $200 OFF! -

At last, after years of secrecy, the **previously unreleased** lesson plans, strategies and playing tactics formerly available only to members of the Cardoza School of Blackjack are now available to the general public - and at substantial savings. **Now**, you can **learn at home,** and at your own convenience. Like the full course given at the school, the home instruction course goes **step-by-ste**p over the winning concepts. We'll take you from layman to **pro.**

MASTER BLACKJACK - Learn what it takes to be a **master player.** Be a **powerhouse**, play with confidence, impunity, and **with the odds** on your side. Learn to be a **big winner** at blackjack.

MAXIMIZE WINNING SESSIONS - You'll **learn how** to take a good winning session and make a **blockbuster** out of it, but just as important, you'll learn to cut your losses. Learn exactly when to end a session. We cover everything from the psychological and emotional aspects of play to altered playing conditions (through the **eye of profitability**) to protection of big wins. The advice here could be worth **hundreds (or thousands) of dollars** in one session alone. Take our guidelines seriously.

ADVANCED STRATEGIES - You'll learn the *latest* in advanced winning strategies. Learn about the **ten-factor**, the **Ace-factor**, the effects of rules variations, how to protect against dealer blackjacks, the winning strategies for single and multiple deck games and how each affects you; the **true count**, the multiple deck true count variations, and much, much more. And, of course, you'll receive the full Cardoza Base Count Strategy package.

$200 OFF - LIMITED OFFER - The Cardoza School of Blackjack home instruction course, retailed at $295 (or $895 if taken at the school) is available here for just $95.

DOUBLE BONUS! - **Rush** your order in **now**, for we're also including, **absolutely free**, the 1,000 and 1,500 word essays, "How to Disguise the Fact that You're an Expert", and "How Not to Get Barred". Among other **inside information** contained here, you'll learn about the psychology of the pit bosses, how they spot counters, how to project a losing image, role playing, and other skills to maximize your profit potential.

To order, send $95 (plus postage and handling) by check or money order to:
Cardoza Publishing, P.O. Box 1500, Cooper Station, New York, NY 10276

SAVE $200!
(regular $295 - Only $95 with coupon)

Order Now! Be a big winner! Please **rush** me the course by mail. I want to join the thousands of successful graduates **winning big money** at blackjack. I understand that the **Double Bonus** essays *and* **free** book will be included **absolutely free.**
Enclosed is a check or money order for $95 (plus postage and handling) made out to:
Cardoza Publishing
P.O. Box 1500, Cooper Station, New York, NY 10276
Call Toll-Free in U.S. & Canada, 1-800-577-WINS
Include $5.00 postage/handling for U.S. orders; $10.00 for Canada/Mexico; HI/AK, other countries, $20.00. Outside U.S., money order payable in U.S. dollars on U.S. bank only.

NAME _____

ADDRESS _____

CITY _____ STATE _____ ZIP _____
Order Now! 30 Day Money Back Guarantee!   AC Poker 2003

153

GRI'S PROFESSIONAL VIDEO POKER STRATEGY
Win Money at Video Poker! With the Odds!

At last, for the **first time,** and for **serious players only,** the GRI **Professional Video Poker** strategy is released so you too can play to win! **You read it right** - this strategy gives you the **mathematical advantage** over the casino and what's more, it's **easy to learn!**

PROFESSIONAL STRATEGY SHOWS YOU HOW TO WIN WITH THE ODDS - This **powerhouse strategy,** played for **big profits** by an **exclusive** circle of **professionals,** people who make their living at the machines, is now made available to you! You too can win - with the odds - and this **winning strategy** shows you how!

HOW TO PLAY FOR A PROFIT - You'll learn the **key factors** to play on a **pro level:** which machines will turn you a profit, break-even and win rates, hands per hour and average win per hour charts, time value, team play and more! You'll also learn big play strategy, alternate jackpot play, high and low jackpot play and key strategies to follow.

WINNING STRATEGIES FOR ALL MACHINES - This **comprehensive, advanced pro package** not only shows you how to win money at the 8-5 progressives, but also, the **winning strategies** for 10s or better, deuces wild, joker's wild, flat-top, progressive and special options features.

BE A WINNER IN JUST ONE DAY - **In just one day**, after learning our strategy, you will have the skills to **consistently win money** at video poker - with the odds. The strategies are easy to use under practical casino conditions.

FREE BONUS - PROFESSIONAL PROFIT EXPECTANCY FORMULA ($15 VALUE) - For serious players, we're including this free bonus essay which explains the professional profit expectancy principles of video poker and how to relate them to real dollars and cents in your game.

To order send just $50 by check or money order to:
Cardoza Publishing, P.O. Box 1500, Cooper Station, New York, NY 10276

GRI'S PROFESSIONAL VIDEO POKER STRATEGY
JUST $50!!! • ORDER NOW!!!

Yes! Please rush me GRI's **Professional Video Poker Strategy** and the **free bonus** ($15 value), **Professional Profit Expectancy Formula.** Enclosed is a check or money order for $50 (plus postage and handling) made out to:
Cardoza Publishing, P.O. Box 1500, Cooper Station, New York, NY 10276

Call Toll-Free in U.S. & Canada, 1-800-577-WINS

Include $5.00 postage/handling for U.S. orders; $10.00 for Canada/Mexico; HI/AK, other countries, $20.00. Outside U.S., money order payable in U.S. dollars on U.S. bank only.

NAME _____

ADDRESS _____

CITY _____ STATE _____ ZIP _____

MC/Visa/Amex Orders By Mail

MC/Visa/Amex# _____ Phone _____

Exp. Date _____ Signature _____

Order Today! 30 Day Money Back Guarantee! AC Poker 2003

GREAT POKER BOOKS
ADD THESE TO YOUR LIBRARY - ORDER NOW!

TOURNAMENT POKER *by Tom McEvoy* - Rated by pros as best book on tournaments ever written, and enthusiastically endorsed by more than 5 world champions, this is a *must* for every player's library. Packed solid with winning strategies for all 11 games in the *World Series of Poker*, with extensive discussions of 7-card stud, limit hold'em, pot and no-limit hold'em, Omaha high-low, re-buy, half-half tournaments, satellites, strategies for each stage of tournaments. Big player profiles. 344 pages, paperback, $39.95.

OMAHA HI-LO POKER *by Shane Smith* - Learn essential winning strategies for beating Omaha high-low; the best starting hands, how to play the flop, turn, and river, how to read the board for both high and low, dangerous draws, plus powerful chapter on winning low-limit tournaments. Learn the differences between Omaha high-low and hold'em strategies. Includes odds charts, glossary, low-limit tips. 84 pages, 8 x 11, spiral bound, $17.95.

7-CARD STUD (THE COMPLETE COURSE IN WINNING AT MEDIUM & LOWER LIMITS) *by Roy West* - Learn the latest strategies for winning at $1-$4 spread-limit up to $10-$20 fixed-limit games. Covers starting hands, 3rd-7th street strategy for playing most hands, overcards, selective aggressiveness, reading hands, secrets of the pros, psychology, more - in a 42 "lesson" informal format. Includes bonus chapter on 7-stud tournament strategy by World Champion Tom McEvoy. 160 pages, paperback, $24.95.

REAL POKER: THE COOK COLLECTION *by Roy Cooke* - The complete collection of *Card Player* poker articles is included in this collection and organized in these categories: Play of Hands; Theory, Strategy and Tactics; Philosophy of Life and the Game; and Miscellaneous Topics. This wealth of poker knowledge is endorsed by stars such as Doyle Brunson, two time world champion, Mike Caro, David Sklansky, and Linda Johnson, publisher of *Card Player*. Lots of practical info! 400 pages, 5 1/2 x 8 1/2, paperback, $19.95.

POKER TOURNAMENT TIPS FROM THE PROS *by Shane Smith* - Essential advice from poker theorists, authors, and tournament winners on the best strategies for winning the big prizes at low-limit re-buy tournaments. Learn the best strategies for each of the four stages of play–opening, middle, late and final–how to avoid 26 potential traps, advice on re-buys, aggressive play, clock-watching, inside moves, top 20 tips for winning tournaments, more. Advice from McEvoy, Caro, Malmuth, Ciaffone, others. 102 pages, 8 1/2 x 11, spiral, $19.95.

WINNERS GUIDE TO TEXAS HOLD 'EM POKER *by Ken Warren* - This comprehensive book shows you how to play every hand from every position with every type of flop. Learn the 14 categories of starting hands, the 10 most common hold 'em tells, how to evaluate a game for profit, and more! Over 50,000 sold. 256 pages, 5 1/2 x 8 1/2, paperback, $14.95.

KEN WARREN TEACHES TEXAS HOLD 'EM *by Ken Warren* - This is a step-by-step manual for making money at hold 'em poker. 42 powerful chapters will teach you one lesson at a time. Great practical advice and concepts accompanied by examples from actual games and how to apply them to your own games. Lessons include: Starting Cards, Playing Position, Which Hands to Play, Raising, Check-raising, Tells, Game and Seat Selection, Dominated Hands, Odds, and more. 416 pages, 6x9, paperback, $24.95.

WINNING POKER FOR THE SERIOUS PLAYER *by Edwin Silberstang* - New Edition! More than 100 actual examples provide tons of advice on beating 7 Card Stud, Texas Hold 'Em, Draw Poker, Loball, High-Low and more than 10 other variations. Silberstang analyzes the essentials of being a great player; reading tells, analyzing tables, playing position, mastering the art of deception, creating fear at the table. Also, psychological tactics, when to play aggressive or slow play, or fold, expert plays, more. Colorful glossary included. 304 pages, 6 x 9, perfect bound, $16.95.

Order Toll-Free 1-800-577-WINS or use order form on page 159

THE CHAMPIONSHIP BOOKS
POWERFUL BOOKS YOU MUST HAVE

CHAMPIONSHIP OMAHA (Omaha High-Low, Pot-limit Omaha, Limit High Omaha) *by T. J. Cloutier & Tom McEvoy.* Clearly-written strategies and powerful advice from Cloutier and McEvoy who have won four World Series of Poker titles in Omaha tournaments. Powerful advice shows you how to win at low-limit and high-stakes games, how to play against loose and tight opponents, and the differing strategies for rebuy and freezeout tournaments. Learn the best starting hands, when slowplaying a big hand is dangerous, what danglers are and why winners don't play them, why pot-limit Omaha is the only poker game where you sometimes fold the nuts on the flop and are correct in doing so and overall, how can you win a lot of money at Omaha! 230 pages, photos, illustrations, $39.95.

CHAMPIONSHIP STUD (Seven-Card Stud, Stud 8/or Better and Razz) *by Dr. Max Stern, Linda Johnson, and Tom McEvoy.* The authors, who have earned millions of dollars in major tournaments and cash games, eight World Series of Poker bracelets and hundreds of other titles in competition against the best players in the world show you the winning strategies for medium-limit side games as well as poker tournaments and a general tournament strategy that is applicable to any form of poker. Includes give-and-take conversations between the authors to give you more than one point of view on how to play poker. 200 pages, hand pictorials, photos. $29.95.

CHAMPIONSHIP HOLD'EM *by T. J. Cloutier & Tom McEvoy.* Hard-hitting hold'em the way it's played *today* in both limit cash games and tournaments. Get killer advice on how to win more money in rammin'-jammin' games, kill-pot, jackpot, shorthanded, and other types of cash games. You'll learn the thinking process before the flop, on the flop, on the turn, and at the river with specific suggestions for what to do when good or bad things happen plus 20 illustrated hands with play-by-play analyses. Specific advice for rocks in tight games, weaklings in loose games, experts in solid games, how hand values change in jackpot games, when you should fold, check, raise, reraise, check-raise, slowplay, bluff, and tournament strategies for small buy-in, big buy-in, rebuy, incremental add-on, satellite and big-field major tournaments. Wow! Easy-to-read and conversational, if you want to become a lifelong winner at limit hold'em, you need this book! 320 Pages, Illustrated, Photos. $39.95

CHAMPIONSHIP NO-LIMIT & POT LIMIT HOLD'EM *by T. J. Cloutier & Tom McEvoy* The definitive guide to winning at two of the world's most exciting poker games! Written by eight time World Champion players T. J. Cloutier (1998 Player of the Year) and Tom McEvoy (the foremost author on tournament strategy) who have won millions of dollars playing no-limit and pot-limit hold'em in cash games and major tournaments around the world. You'll get all the answers here - no holds barred - to your most important questions: How do you get inside your opponents' heads and learn how to beat them at their own game? How can you tell how much to bet, raise, and reraise in no-limit hold'em? When can you bluff? How do you set up your opponents in pot-limit hold'em so that you can win a monster pot? What are the best strategies for winning no-limit and pot-limit tournaments, satellites, and supersatellites? You get rock-solid and inspired advice from two of the most recognizable figures in poker — advice that you can bank on. If you want to become a winning player, a champion, you must have this book. 209 pages, paperback, illustrations, photos. $39.95

Order Toll-Free 1-800-577-WINS or use order form on page 159

VIDEOS BY MIKE CARO
THE MAD GENIUS OF POKER

CARO'S PRO POKER TELLS

The long-awaited two-video set is a powerful scientific course on how to use your opponents' gestures, words and body language to read their hands and win all their money. These carefully guarded poker secrets, filmed with 63 poker notables, will revolutionize your game. It reveals when opponents are bluffing, when they aren't, and why. Knowing what your opponent's gestures mean, and protecting them from knowing yours, gives you a huge winning edge. *An absolute must buy!* $59.95.

CARO'S MAJOR POKER SEMINAR

The legendary "Mad Genius" is at it again, giving poker advice in VHS format. This new tape is based on the inaugural class at Mike Caro University of Poker, Gaming and Life strategy. The material given on this tape is based on many fundamentals introduced in Caro's books, papers, and articles and is prepared in such a way that reinforces concepts old and new. Caro's style is easy-going but intense with key concepts stressed and repeated. This tape will improve your play. 60 Minutes. $24.95.

CARO'S POWER POKER SEMINAR

This powerful video shows you how to win big money using the little-known concepts of world champion players. This advice will be worth thousands of dollars to you every year, even more if you're a big money player! After 15 years of refusing to allow his seminars to be filmed, Caro presents entertaining but serious coverage of his long-guarded secrets. Contains the most profitable poker advice ever put on video. 62 Minutes! $39.95.

Order Toll-Free 1-800-577-WINS or use order form on page 159

CARDOZA PUBLISHING ONLINE

For the latest in poker, gambling, chess, backgammon, and games
by the world's top authorities and writers

www.cardozapub.com

To find out about our latest publications and products, to order books and software from third parties, or simply to keep aware of our latest activities in the world or poker, gambling, and other games of chance and skill:

1. Go online: www.cardozapub.com
2. Use E-Mail: cardozapub@aol.com
3. Call toll free: 800-577-WINS (800-577-9467)

DOYLE BRUNSON'S SUPER SYSTEM
A COURSE IN POKER POWER!
by World Champion Doyle Brunson

CONSIDERED BY PROS THE BEST POKER BOOK EVER WRITTEN

This is the **classic** book on every major no-limit game played today and is considered by the pros to be one of the **best books ever written** on poker! **Jam-packed** with **advanced strategies**, theories, tactics and money-making techniques - no serious poker player can afford to be without this **essential** book! Hardbound, and packed with 605 pages of hard-hitting information, this is truly a **must-buy** for aspiring pros. Includes 50 pages of the most precise poker statistics ever published!

CHAPTERS WRITTEN BY GAME'S SUPERSTARS

The best theorists and poker players in the world, Dave Sklansky, Mike Caro, Chip Reese, Bobby Baldwin and Doyle Brunson, a **book by champions for aspiring pros** - cover the **essential** strategies and **advanced play** in their respective specialties. Three world champions and two master theorists and players provide non-nonsense winning advice on making money at the tables.

LEARN WINNING STRATEGIES FOR THE MAJOR POKER GAMES

The important money games today are covered in depth by these **poker superstars**. You'll learn seven-card stud, draw poker, lowball, seven-card low stud (razz), high-low split (cards speak) and high-low declare; and the most popular game in the country today, hold'em (limit and no-limit). Each game is covered in detail with the **important winning concepts** and strategies clearly explained so that anyone can become a **bigger money** winner.

SERIOUS POKER PLAYERS MUST HAVE THIS BOOK

This is **mandatory reading** for aspiring poker pros, players planning to enter tournaments, players ready to play no-limit. *Doyle Brunson's Super System* is also ideal for average players seeking to move to higher stakes games for bigger wins and more challenges.

To order, send $29.95 by check or money order to <u>Cardoza Publishing</u>

DOYLE BRUNSON'S SUPER SYSTEM - NOW JUST $29.95!

Yes! Please **rush** me Doyle Brunson's Super System - the 624-page masterpiece (**now in paperback!**) for serious poker players. Enclosed is a check or money order for $29.95 (plus postage and handling) made out to:

Cardoza Publishing, P.O. Box 1500, Cooper Station, New York, NY 10276

Call Toll-Free in U.S. & Canada, 1-800-577-WINS

Include $7.00 postage/handling for U.S. orders; $17.00 for Canada/Mexico; HI/AK, other countries, $27.00. Outside U.S., money order payable in U.S. dollars on U.S. bank only.

NAME _____

ADDRESS _____

CITY _____ STATE _____ ZIP _____

MC/Visa/Amex Orders By Mail

MC/Visa/Amex# _____ Phone _____

Exp. Date _____ Signature _____

Order Today! 30 Day Money Back Guarantee!   AC Poker 2003

BOOKS BY MIKE CARO
THE MAD GENIUS OF POKER

CARO'S BOOK OF TELLS (THE BODY LANGUAGE OF POKER) - Finally! Mike Caro's classic book is now revised and back in print! This long-awaited revision by the Mad Genius of Poker takes a detailed look at the art and science of tells, the physical mannerisms which giveaway a player's hand. Featuring photo illustrations of poker players in action along with Caro's explanations about when players are bluffing and when they're not, these powerful eye-opening ideas can give you the decisive edge at the table! This invaluable book should be in every player's library! 352 pages! $24.95.

CARO'S GUIDE TO DOYLE BRUNSON'S SUPER SYSTEM - Working with World Champion Doyle Brunson, the legendary Mike Caro has created a fresh look to the "Bible" of all poker books, adding new and personal insights that help you understand the original work. Caro breaks 36 concepts into either "Analysis, Commentary, Concept, Mission, Play-By-Play, Psychology, Statistics, Story, or Strategy. Lots of illustrations and winning concepts give even more value to this great work. 86 pages, 8 1/2 x 11, stapled. $19.95.

CARO'S FUNDAMENTAL SECRETS OF WINNING POKER -The world's foremost poker theoretician and strategist presents the essential strategies, concepts, and secret winning plays that comprise the very foundation of winning poker play. Shows how to win more from weak players, equalize stronger players, bluff a bluffer, win big pots, where to sit against weak players, the six factors of strategic table image. Includes selected tips on hold 'em, 7 stud, draw, lowball, tournaments, more. 160 Pages, 5 1/2 x 8 1/2, perfect bound, $9.95.

Call Toll Free (800)577-WINS or Use Coupon Below to Order Books, Videos & Software

BECOME A BETTER POKER PLAYER!

YES! I want to be a winner! Rush me the following items: (Write in choices below):

Quantity	Your Book Order		Price	

MAKE CHECKS TO:	Subtotal		
Cardoza Publishing	Postage/Handling: First Item	$5	00
P. O. Box 1500			
New York, NY 10276	Additional Postage		
CHARGE BY PHONE:	Total Amount Due		
Toll-Free: 1-800-577-WINS			
E-Mail Orders: cardozapub@aol.com			

SHIPPING CHARGES: For US orders, include $5.00 postage/handling 1st book ordered; for each additional book, add $1.00. For Canada/Mexico, double above amounts, quadruple (4X) for all other countries. Orders outside U.S., money order payable in U.S. dollars on U.S. bank only.

NAME _____

ADDRESS _____

CITY _____ STATE _____ ZIP _____

30 day money back guarantee!   AC Poker 2003

POWERFUL POKER SIMULATIONS

A MUST FOR SERIOUS PLAYERS WITH A COMPUTER!
IBM compatibles CD ROM Windows 3.1, 95, and 98 - Full Color Graphics

Play interactive poker against these **incredible** full color poker simulation programs - they're the absolute **best** method to improve game. *Computer players act like real players.* All games let you set the limits and rake, have fully programmable players, adjustable lineup, stat tracking, and Hand Analyzer for starting hands. MIke Caro, the world's foremost poker theoretician says, *"Amazing...A steal for under $500...get it, it's great."* Includes *free telephone support.* **New Feature!** - "Smart advisor" gives expert advice for *every* play in *every* game!

1. TURBO TEXAS HOLD'EM FOR WINDOWS - $89.95 - Choose which players, how many, 2-10, you want to play, create loose/tight game, control check-raising, bluffing, position, sensitivity to pot odds, more! Also, instant replay, pop-up odds, Professional Advisor, keeps track of play statistics. Free bonus: *Hold'em Hand Analyzer* analyzes all 169 pocket hands in detail, their win rates under any conditions you set. Caro says this *"hold'em software is the most powerful ever created."* Great product!

2. TURBO SEVEN-CARD STUD FOR WINDOWS - $89.95 - *Create any conditions of play,* choose number of players (2-8), bet amounts, fixed or spread limit, bring-in method, tight/ loose conditions, position, reaction to board, number of dead cards, stack deck to create special conditions, instant replay. Terrific stat reporting includes analysis of starting cards, 3-D bar charts, graphs. Play interactively, run high speed simulation to test strategies. *Hand Analyzer* analyzes starting hands in detail. Wow!

3. TURBO OMAHA HIGH-LOW SPLIT FOR WINDOWS - $89.95 -Specify any playing conditions; betting limits, number of raises, blind structures, button position, aggressiveness/ passiveness of opponents, number of players (2-10), types of hands dealt, blinds, position, board reaction, specify flop, turn, river cards! Choose opponents, use provided point count or create your own. Statistical reporting, instant replay, pop-up odds, high speed simulation to test strategies, amazing Hand Analyzer, much more!

4. TURBO OMAHA HIGH FOR WINDOWS - $89.95 - Same features as above, but tailored for the Omaha High-only game. Caro says program is *"an electrifying research tool...it can clearly be worth thousands of dollars to any serious player.* A must for Omaha High players.

5. TURBO 7 STUD 8 OR BETTER - $89.95 - Brand new with all the features you expect from the Wilson Turbo products: the latest artificial intelligence, instant advice and exact odds, play versus 2-7 opponents, enhanced data charts that can be exported or printed, the ability to fold out of turn and immediately go to the next hand, ability to peek at opponents hand, optional warning mode that warns you if a play disagrees with the advisor, and automatic testing mode that can run up to 50 tests unattended. Challenge tough computer players who vary their styles for a truly great poker game.

6. TOURNAMENT TEXAS HOLD'EM - $59.95

Set-up for tournament practice and play, this realistic simulation pits you against celebrity look-alikes. Tons of options let you control tournament size with 10 to 300 entrants, select limits, ante, rake, blind structures, freezeouts, number of rebuys and competition level of opponents - average, tough, or toughest. Pop-up status report shows how you're doing vs. the competition. Save tournaments in progress to play again later. Additional feature allows you to quickly finish a folded hand and go on to the next.

Order Toll-Free 1-800-577-WINS or use order form on page 159